DAVID M. SCHWARZ ARCHITECTS

FORTY YEARS

DAVID M. SCHWARZ ARCHITECTS

FORTY YEARS

images
Publishing

CVS

CONTENTS

ABOUT THE AUTHOR

Craig P. Williams has been associated with David M. Schwarz Architects for forty-five years. Starting in March 1979 during spring break from the University of Maryland School of Architecture, he progressed from intern to job captain to project architect to project manager, and finally to principal. He served in those capacities on many of the firm's projects presented in this volume. Those he is most proud of include the Ballpark in Arlington, Bass Hall, 1133 Connecticut Avenue, Severance Hall, the American Airlines Center, Schermerhorn Symphony Center, Sid Richardson Museum and the Charleston Gaillard Center.

He has also worked on several historic restorations/renovations and many one-off, single-family residential projects, not detailed in this book, in places far and wide, including Washington, D.C.; Seal Harbor, Maine; White Post, Virginia; Fort Worth, Texas; and Moab, Utah.

At the end of 2016, Williams entered a new phase at the firm. No longer working full time, he stepped back from direct project management to spend more time on other interests. As of this writing, he is still involved in firm management, advising on legal matters, ongoing business development, maintaining client relationships, and at-large design critiques. He also serves as a design, technical, and history resource for the firm. When not working at the firm, Williams is the programmer, host, and DJ of a morning jazz radio program on WPFW, 89.3FM in Washington, D.C. and he volunteers at Humane Rescue Alliance—where he and his wife, Kimberly Schenck, were adopted by Stripe, a sweet, lovable, and slightly overly rambunctious Pit-mix puppy. In addition to spending time with Kim and Stripe, in his remaining "spare time" Williams explores other hobbies and diversions including driving his 1971 Lancia Fulvia Italian rally car, cooking, wine and whiskey, vacuum-tube and LP audio equipment, gardening, photography, and travel.

ABOUT THE BOOK

All essays in this book are based either on Craig P. Williams's firsthand recollections or direct conversations with his colleagues who worked on these projects. Rather than writing lengthy, detailed, architectural descriptions, he purposely chose to use a more narrative prose, hoping to enlighten readers about the human backstories behind how these buildings came to be. Along with his colleagues who contributed to the making of this book, he has chosen to let the pictures speak for themselves about the quality of the work. Furthermore, he has consciously attempted to avoid "archispeak," that professional jargon that architects overuse to a fault. He apologizes in advance to readers should they find any.

THANKS

First and foremost, Craig P. Williams wishes to thank the firm's clients without whom none of these projects would have happened. Next he wishes to thank founding principal and chairperson, David M. Schwarz, for over four decades of mentorship, collaboration, and friendship. He also wishes to thank the firm's other principals, Michael Swartz, Gregory Hoss, and Steve Knight; retired Principal Emeritus Thomas H. Greene; the firm's talented associates; and all other teammates who have worked tirelessly, with dedication and comradery, to make these projects the best they could be in their time. He also wishes to thank all those who have written for monographs about the firm, the inhouse authors of project descriptions, and our business development and marketing personnel over the years. Finally, a special shout-out goes to Associate and Development Derek Marks, who served as project manager for this enormous undertaking.

FOREWORD

Andres Duany and Lizz Plater-Zyberk

The work of David M. Schwarz's firm has been extensively and beautifully documented in the series of prior volumes that emerged chronologically. This volume is different—it is a cross-section of the oeuvre, a specific representation of the firm. It can be assumed to have a purpose beyond documentation, and perhaps a different spirit as David's colleagues look back on the work with the perspective of many eyes over several decades.

We can perhaps add an outsider's perception. Among the monographs published by the major traditionalist firms, this one stands out for intriguing juxtapositions. Let us begin with the firm's original name, David M. Schwarz Architectural Services. This most utilitarian, unpretentious of labels contradicts the talent that has designed some of the most ambitious buildings of our time. These civic buildings are great - they are enormous and architecturally extravagant, skillfully interpreting tradition at a contemporary scale—but more importantly they are cultural tours de force, elevating the institutions and the cities they represent. They recall a neglected history of similar American ambition.

The two Gothic colleges for Vanderbilt—for which four are planned—are as ambitious as those of Yale a century ago—an institution that was then intellectually accomplished, but embodied in a campus so provincial and disjointed that this excellence was not manifest until the campus also expressed it. It is now Vanderbilt's time to confirm physically its intellectual status, and David with the Board of Trustees understand this better than anyone.

The great concert halls for Fort Worth, Nashville, and Charleston may be as expected of a nation with the boundless aspiration of raw cities like Pasadena, when Arthur Brown's great Civic Center was built. And indeed, they remind us of the greatest of all visions, classical Washington, which utterly transcended its reality as a city that was still a pestilential conglomeration of ramshackle wood buildings.

And then the stadia across the south, built to confirm the cultural and economic importance of those cities. The self-effacing Architectural Services has many times justified the extravagant visions of community leaders who risked all had they not succeeded. They trusted David and were justified in doing so.

At the level of detail: there is the radical, even surreal, phenomenon of a heedlessly rich ornamental program from architects led by a personage so matter-of-fact that one would have rather expected a Gropius result. We have remarked on this quiet confidence since our days as classmates. We still remember the shocking audacity of the young David presenting a Gothic extension for the Peabody Museum. This at the center of the Yale campus, the Valhalla of the Gothic masters, inviting comparison with James Gamble Rogers and Ralph Adams Cram. This aplomb served well to avoid the weakness of recent lightly referential predecessors at Yale, as well as the overwrought Gothic that followed.

Then there is the contradiction of a person who, from observation, seems to have quite a lot of free time, and yet we know that he considers every detail of the firm's enormous production. This we can only understand in relation to the seasoned younger partners and colleagues. They stand in contrast to most of the traditional architecture today, which increases in academic expertise but not in the creativity that normally accompanies seasoned mastery. Our cohort remains fearfully conservative while crafting their precious objects, while David takes risks at the very edge of the precipice. That he rarely loses control we suspect may be because he is unusually conversant in the disciplines of urbanism.

One last observation deserving of note—in this case not a contradiction or surprising at all. These buildings of ambition and complexity were brought to reality with an extraordinary set of colleagues. This confirms that David has also created a working culture across several generations, which will no doubt continue to make important contributions. Astutely, he has surrounded himself with talent—the best clients, the best collaborators, builders, managers, and professional colleagues.

FORTY YEARS

David Schwarz

This book presents forty years of David M. Schwarz Architects' work. It includes projects from our formative years and many from the recent past. These include the Charleston Gaillard Center, the performing arts center that opened in 2015, and Rothschild College, the third of four residential colleges we have designed for Vanderbilt University which opened in the Fall of 2020.

Our practice is an unusual one. Most firms "specialize" in particular building types. We aggressively do not. We have come to that through diverse forces. I have selected four early commissions to demonstrate the common threads that shape our work.

Putting together this book has been an interesting experience for me. I am bad with dates, but I am good at remembering our buildings and what was happening in my life as we designed them. The firm has organized our previous monographs chronologically—a useful tool when someone asks me for the date of one event or another. This book, however, presents our work by building type. As I look through it, I think differently about our work. Rather than seeing a personal narrative, I see diverse projects knit together by a maxim and set of principles that my partners, associates, and I have used to shape our work.

We have developed the concept of the "passive user." Our buildings are experienced by a multiplicity of people, most of whom never set foot in them. They either walk or drive past them, sometimes on a daily basis, and have no choice but to experience them. We believe that we, as architects, have a responsibility to them as well, and want our buildings to enrich their lives.

I completed my undergraduate education at St. John's College in Annapolis, Maryland. The college, then and now, teaches through a Great Books program and embraces the maxim that a well-educated person can teach anything and will acquire a lifelong commitment to the pursuit of knowledge. Those persons are, per the College's Statement of the Program of Instruction, "well-equipped to master the specific skills of any calling." I embraced this maxim and adapted it to my own interests. A good designer, per my interpretation, can design anything. The firm continues to prove this true through its diverse body of work.

Our work is guided by a set of first principles. They are that good design is informed by context, is scaled to the pedestrian, and is styled in a way that represents the greatest aspirations of the client. People meet on the sidewalks, not in their cars. And people-watching remains the most popular sport in America. These principles were learned working on early commissions in Washington, D.C., the city to which I moved after graduating from Yale's Master of Architecture program and working for several years at firms in New York.

The office began, as many do, by designing kitchen renovations and decks in the District. We eventually graduated to townhouse renovations. A couple of years on, we graduated to multifamily residential buildings and then received a commission for our first new-construction commercial building on Connecticut Avenue.

At the time, the D.C. government and the United States government passed pieces of legislation that greatly impacted development. The D.C. government passed one of the most sweeping historic preservation laws of any place in the United States, and the federal government passed the Tax Act of 1984, a law that permitted the very accelerated, non-recapturable depreciation for the restoration/renovation of historic structures.

Our client was a partner in a very prominent D.C. law firm. He invested in real estate as a way of diversifying his investment portfolio. With the passage of these two laws, he saw an opportunity to create a small cottage industry. He sold his partners the tax losses and used the cash to begin to build a mini real-estate empire.

For us, this was a very important step in our learning process. D.C. had many historic districts. We had to carefully study them when building in them. We had to understand what was important to those neighborhoods. We began to study how each building became a building block that made neighborhoods and then how neighborhoods formed towns and cities. This gave us a much greater awareness of context and was the origin of our becoming committed to "context" in all our design work.

What finally permitted us to expand our geographic footprint was a historic preservation case in Fort Worth, Texas. I got a call from a local who was suing the state government to block the expansion of an elevated highway that ran through downtown Fort Worth; I had been recommended as an expert witness. I declined, saying that I have always thought that when one is paid to be an expert witness, the testimony is suspect. I told him we were a small, not particularly well-funded architecture firm and that we could simply not take a pro-bono case that far away.

He then asked me if I would at least come to look at his problem. I had never been to Texas and a free trip to see it sounded like a pretty good idea. So, I went. Once I saw the problem, I thought that it was such an important issue that I had to say yes. We worked through terms wherein I could study the impact of elevated freeways on urban centers, form an independent perspective, and speak authoritatively when called upon to make a compelling presentation. Whether I knew it or not then, this would be the beginning of a long relationship.

I have selected four Texas projects that occurred in quick succession to expand upon context as it relates to our first principles. They are Cook Children's Medical Center, The Ballpark in Arlington, Bass Hall, and Southlake Town Square. Whereas context as it applied to our early practice in D.C. often related to the city's urban fabric, context as it applies to these commissions is broader.

Our client won the aforementioned lawsuit and invited us back to Fort Worth to interview for a new children's hospital. He was the Chairman of the Board of Fort Worth Children's Medical Center, which was merging with Cook Children's Hospital to form the new Cook Children's Medical Center. To date, we had not designed a hospital, but the chairman believed we could bring a fresh perspective. His faith in us was not shared by the rest of the board, most of whom wanted to hire a firm with extensive hospital experience. We proposed an arrangement under which we would design the master plan, the building exteriors and patient-and-parent oriented interiors. We would partner with a hospital architect who would design the technical parts of the work and the back-of-house spaces. Our proposal was declined.

About a year later I got a call from the chairman asking me back to Fort Worth. A hospital specialist had been hired to design the new building. He showed me the schematic plans for the proposed campus and pressed me on my thoughts. I offered that the spaces were "quite well organized." Pressed on how it looked, I decided to abandon caution and tell him I thought it looked quite ugly and might be frightening to children. He replied, "I agree with you. I have a thesis that given equal medical care, parents will take their children to the nicer place to be, and this will not accomplish that." We returned to our original proposal and we have had a building in design or under construction on the Cook campus since 1985. The net result is that the complex is very "cohesive" and easy to understand. The original building was approximately 400,000 square feet and the complex is now over 1,800,000 square feet.

Cook Children's Medical Center confirmed the Chairman's intuition and validated our core principle that good design is informed by context. We knew that we were designing to the context of the user: patients and their parents. What surprised both of us was the overwhelmingly positive response from doctors, nurses, and the medical staff who chose to work at Cook over comparable institutions. Given equal pay, people will work in the nicer place to be. Our maxim that a good designer could design anything had also been proven true. As a result, we were able to begin to convince people that hiring us because we had never designed their project type before was not a risk. Rather, we could bring "fresh take" and create a place that was uniquely theirs.

This validation of our approach to the practice of architecture was liberating to me. Not only because we would not have to design the same building type repeatedly, but also because it gave us the license to "learn" to design any building type. We had to learn a little bit about a lot of things. Not only would I be much happier but so would everyone else in the office. We all would constantly learn new things and it would make for a very interesting work environment. The hospital led directly to our next large project: The Ballpark in Arlington for the Texas Rangers Baseball Team. It was common knowledge that the Rangers were going to build a new ballpark and that the team's president intended to hold a design competition. I, like several other architects, tried to convince him to save some time and money by skipping the competition and just hiring us. We had a cordial conversation but, in the end, he said, "Thank you very much, David. I think I will hold my design competition." I responded we would likely decline to enter as competitions were expensive and we were still a young firm.

He assembled a list of around twenty-two firms. There were starchitects, firms that specialized in "sports architecture," and a group of what he called "dark horses." The latter were firms he found interesting but had no real credentials to show they could design a ballpark. We were added at the last moment because the president's son had just spent some time at Cook. He was aware it was the first (and only) hospital we had designed. He liked the building so much that he was curious how we would approach a ballpark.

The president invited all firms on the list to come to the site and speak with members of the team. I went because I was in town anyway. One of the questions I asked the president was, "What color do you think of when you think about baseball?" His answer was sepia. That told me everything I needed to know to design the new ballpark. His view of baseball was nostalgic, which convinced me our response should be as well. The site was in the middle of a vast sea of surface parking lots so there was no physical context to which we could relate. We decided to focus on the history of baseball and the history of Texas architecture as our context.

We studied ballparks extensively, both for how they looked and for how they worked. We looked for things we liked and for things we thought could be done better. As baseball is a sport with a rich history, we decided we would "quote" other ballparks as we prepared our submission. Our Home Run Porch, for instance was a direct quote from Detroit. The right field wall pays tribute to the Green Monster in

Boston. We talked to everyone we could find in the baseball world and learned about the business and the ceremony of baseball.

The name of the team is the Texas Rangers, not the Dallas or Fort Worth Rangers. Texas is a place where people have moved from all over the country. So, we chose the whole state as our inspiration. The ballpark architecture takes its cues from the State House in Austin, some parts of the Rice University Campus, as well as a host of other buildings throughout the state. The "Lone Star" is used as a motif throughout the ballpark. Outside, bas-relief panels pay tribute to the actual Texas Rangers as well as the baseball team.

Luckily for us, we were right and ended up being selected to design the new ballpark. We have always been interested in designing "places for people." The ballpark is certainly one. We have always believed architecture can cause people to separate or bring them together. The building was designed to give all ticket holders—from chairman of the board through factory line worker—an equally memorable experience. On opening day, the president's speech talked largely of the importance of architecture. I was amazed. The president of a baseball team focusing on architecture? Who would have thought? The ballpark has become a much-loved facility in North Texas. So much so that when new owners wanted to build a new ballpark, they were forced to commit to keeping the old ballpark up and functioning in order to pass their bond issue.

Directly after the ballpark was completed, we were hired to design a new concert hall for Fort Worth. At the behest of the client, we had been developing a master plan for the city's urban core. That client's goal was to produce a cultural focus for downtown—a performing arts venue that would serve all of Fort Worth—and be a place for "The People." This was important to us as well. Downtowns serve as the "front porch" for a communities. It is the only place where everyone comes. It is where people go to watch the world go by. We wanted to embrace the city's population and have them view this as their place. We suggested that since performance halls are dark most days of the week, a site on the edge of downtown rather than in the center would be appropriate. We have always believed that there are different categories of buildings, that most buildings are "fabric buildings" and ought to contribute to the creation of a neighborhood. But some buildings are so special and unique that they ought to be "object buildings" as they serve and help to define the community writ large. The historic context of Fort Worth is mostly two- and three-story brick buildings. There are also a number of large brick office buildings built in the 1920s and 1930s and massive skyscrapers built primarily out of glass and steel. We ignored this context and decided that the most important context was the work that was going to be performed inside. We wanted our building to reflect the grandeur and ceremony of the halls for which the performances were composed.

Two massive angels project from the main façade. Their bodies lean well over the sidewalk and their trumpets reach to the middle of the street, making the building visible from quite a distance east and west. We created two corner entrances facing where most people came from. This permitted us to create four large windows on the center of the front façade opening onto the main lobby. Opposite the hall, we designed a restaurant that invites diners to be passive users and watch the spectacle from across the street. These various features allowed us to knit the building into the life of downtown Fort Worth in ways that make the hall central to downtown's vitality without impacting the feel of the city from nine to five.

Here again, we worked to make every patron's experience a wonderful one. A great part of the performing arts is the ceremony. There is an anticipation when one enters the building, excitement in the procession to the hall itself, and a grand moment when one walks into the hall. We wanted to make it a memorable experience no matter what ticket price one had. One lesson we learned from the design of the ballpark was that unusual seats made a great addition. So, we created two "piano boxes" (so called because of their shape) which were quite high and projected far into the room. As a result, the person is very far forward and looks down on the stage. Details like these make the hall unique.

Bass Hall has been a great success. It brings over half a million people to downtown every year and has hosted thousands of performances. Loren Maazel, maestro of the New York Philharmonic Orchestra, said after performing in it, "This is exactly what we need in New York City." The hall was built when there were telephone books. At that time, we viewed the greatest award we could win was to be put on the cover of the telephone book. When that happens, it signifies the community has chosen that building to be a symbol of themselves and their city. That is what happened in the case of Bass Hall.

The other project on which we were working at that time was Southlake Town Square. Names like this usually denote some sort of shopping center trying to masquerade as a town. This was not the case here. Southlake Town Square was the first opportunity we had to create what we thought a town should be from "whole cloth." We committed to the pedestrian scale and walkable streets, along with ample parks and recreational areas.

When I first arrived in Texas, a client invited me to a meeting followed by a lunch. After the meeting, we took the elevator down from his thirty-first-floor office. I walked toward the front door, and he walked toward the parking garage. Lunch was two blocks away. Sensing my confusion he said, "One of the first things you need to learn David, is that Texans don't walk." I kept rolling it over in mind and, after three months, concluded that architects, planners, and developers had not given Texans places worth walking since World War II.

Prior to our arrival, the City of Southlake, Texas, had developed similarly to many twentieth-century suburbs. There was a mass of strip centers to provide for people's daily needs but no focus to the area. The town's government was enlightened enough to know that this was not what they wanted for their community. The city designated over 100 acres as a town center, but there was no description within the code as to what that meant. We were hired to develop a master plan, author a zoning code, and create a set of design guidelines. Our mission was to prove that Texans would walk if we gave them places worth walking.

We looked to the context of the traditional town to inform our efforts. We wanted a mix of uses including housing, office, and retail. At the time, Southlake was planning a new city hall in a strip center. Texas has a storied tradition of locating an important civic structure in the center of town and on a town square. We proposed following this precedent. The city hall, we argued should be sited within our plan and located on "Town Square," hence the name of the development. Once the plan was ratified by the city council, we were hired to begin the vertical development. There was so much to design that within our office we divided the project into much smaller parts and put together different teams to work on different parts of it. The teams were not allowed to look at each other's work. We hired a series of outside architects to work on parts of it as well. Only I and the project manager had a view of the whole project. The result is a collection of quite different yet highly sympathetic buildings, all styled to the aspirations of the client. We have been adding to it since 1996.

We have learned that architecture is a marketing tool. Many of Southlake's residents are transplants from around the country. We endeavored to design the vertical development of Southlake Town Square in a series of styles that people would find sympathetic, familiar, and interesting, regardless of where they were from. One of the nation's largest shopping-center developers asked us to come to their office and give a presentation. When we were done, one of the partners said, "I don't get this. I cannot see how this possibly could work. Where are your anchors?" I responded, "The park is an anchor as are all the benches. The coffee shop and ice cream parlor are anchors." I then went back to the slides to show all the mothers congregating with strollers in the morning. And, in the afternoon, all the twenty-somethings walking up and down the sidewalks.

In many ways, Southlake proved the chairman's thesis that all else being equal—whether in reference to pediatric health care or lifestyle—the quality of experience really does affect people's choices. People vote for the better place with their feet.

I hope this explanation helps you to understand the following pages. We are humanists and care greatly about creating the best possible spaces we can. In these pages, one can see how our development as a firm has affected the building types we have designed over time. As we look toward the coming years, we are planning for a brand-new slate of performing arts, higher education, mixed-use, and civic projects. Abiding by the principles we've honed over our first four decades, my partners, associates, and I know that we can create new places that make people's lives better, richer, and happier. In closing, I want to express my gratitude to my partners, Gregory Hoss, Craig Williams, Michael Swartz, and Steve Knight as well as Associate Derek Marks for the effort they have put into making this book the best it can be. I would also like to acknowledge all those who have made our buildings happen, from our clients to our consultants, craftsmen, and the builders who have constructed them. Perhaps, most importantly, I want to thank all the people who make up our firm including my partners, our ten associates, and the staff members. Their collaborative contributions have made the projects represented herein a reality.

SPORTS & ENTERTAINMENT

THE BALLPARK
IN
ARLINGTON
HOME PLATE
TICKETS

THE BALLPARK IN ARLINGTON

Arlington, Texas, 1991
Client: The Texas Rangers Baseball Club

When the Texas Rangers Baseball Club sent a Request for Proposals (RFP) to twenty-two architectural firms from across the country, everyone realized it was a thinly veiled invitation to participate in a design competition. The ball club sent the RFP to the major sports architects, large well-respected design firms, some local favorites and a handful of dark-horse candidates. After the fact, David M. Schwarz Architects learned that the Rangers' president, Ambassador Thomas Schieffer, considered them somewhere between a local favorite and a dark horse. The firm came to his attention when his son spent weeks in the Schwarz-designed Cook Children's Medical Center (see page 198).

Having played in an inadequate converted minor-league stadium for nearly two decades, the Rangers were quite clear on their vision for a new ballpark. How to give that vision form was the challenge. After reading the RFP, which articulated that vision well, Mr. Schwarz declared, "I know how to win this." One had to simply appeal to Texans' strong sense of pride and their never-ending desire for profit. Additionally, it was clear that Ambassador Schieffer, the author of the RFP, was both a student of the game's history and a fan of its nostalgia and memories. The firm geared its response to play off those sentiments.

To address the issue of Texan pride, the firm carefully studied the history of the Texas Rangers, both the twenty-year history of the ball team and the more than 150 years of the law enforcement agency. They also utilized their vast knowledge of Texas's architectural history. The RFP stressed that the team was the Texas Rangers, not the Arlington Rangers or the Dallas–Fort Worth Rangers. The Schwarz team's concept designs included nods to the Texas Capitol and governor's mansion in Austin, buildings at Rice University in Houston, and the Tarrant County Courthouse in Fort Worth. Baseball is a sport steeped in its own history. The competition entry also included tributes to landmark ballparks of yesteryear, which the architect went on to refine in the final design. For example, Home Run Porch was an homage to the old Tiger Stadium in Detroit. David M. Schwarz Architects presented on the final day of four, and while it took weeks for the Rangers to publicly announce it, they prevailed. Long after the fact, one member of the selection committee revealed that the committee let out a collective sigh of relief when Mr. Schwarz unveiled the concept elevation replete with Texas granite, longhorns, and lone stars.

To address the profit-making needs of the club, the firm produced both short- and long-term master plans of the entire 270 acres under the Rangers' control, showing how, over time, the club could maximize the value of the land. Additionally, the firm learned from a rival team president everything about the five major revenue streams in baseball. Their competition entry included elements designed to maximize those income streams: ticket sales, outdoor advertising, broadcast rights, concessions, and parking. They continued to develop all of these as their design efforts progressed. For instance, they employed tree-lined paths to provide shade and break up seas of parking; they carefully integrated advertising locations so that ownership would not allow advertisers to place ads wherever they wanted; and they designed specific

camera positions that would not interfere with fans' views. Furthermore, the architects placed the main novelty store and supplementary novelty stands where a parent's resistance to a child's pleadings would be most diminished.

Having given preliminary form to the vision, then came the task of making the form a reality. From the 1960s through 1980s, new baseball facilities were round multisport stadiums built in a sea of parking. While what is generally considered the first of many nostalgic ballparks was under construction in Baltimore, that was not the precedent for The Ballpark in Arlington—the precedent was the Rangers' vision. Furthermore, the Schwarz team wanted more than a stadium with an old-timey, ballpark, stage-set façade. This ballpark would be a real building for people, inside and out. They wanted a building that would be reviewed by architecture critics as well as sports writers, which occurred when the architecture critic from the *New York Times* wrote about it shortly after its completion. The firm accomplished this by placing a seating bowl, optimized for the fans, within an almost square brick and granite edifice of over 800 feet per side. Between the bowl and the building, well-defined and interconnected concourses provide an ample array of patron amenities that generate equally plentiful income for the club. An outer concourse, which follows the orthogonal geometry of the façades, serves as express circulation. An inner concourse, which follows the seating bowl geometry, provides easy access to the concessions, restrooms, and vomitoria.

When completed, the ballpark represented the firm's most thorough use, to that date, of iconographic imagery as the source of architectural detail and ornament. Lone stars appear in both the exterior and interior, from façade medallions to truss elements, railings, and seat-end stanchions. Around the entire perimeter, the history of the Texas Rangers (again, both ball players and lawmen) is portrayed in bas-relief panels. Portraits of hall-of-famers are used to designate the private suites. Finally, they used the tools of the trade—balls and bats—in signage and light fixtures.

page 18: Home plate gate detail
above: Local iconography used as ornament
opposite (clockwise from top): Stadium seen from Richard Greene Linear Park; Bas-relief panel detail; Baseball Hall of Fame iconography; Diamond Stadium Club; Lower deck main concourse

"We wanted to build a ballpark that people, when they came into it would remember it, and when they saw it on television would remember it and instantly know where they were."

—Tom Schieffer

Partner-in-Charge, Ballpark Development Group

BLOCKBUSTER VIDEO
First Interstate
FINA
Lite
Coca-Cola
INCREDIBLE
UNIVERSE
Electronics-Appliances-Comp

opposite: Center field office building
clockwise from top left: View down first-base line; Steel frame detail; Seating detail
left: Dr Pepper Youth Ballpark
following: Aerial view

SOUTHWEST AIRLINES
TARGET

Budweiser

TICKETS

ESPN'S WIDE WORLD OF SPORTS COMPLEX

Lake Buena Vista, Florida, 1994
Client: Disney Development Company

David M. Schwarz Architects first met executives of the Walt Disney Company and Disney Development Company when their loyal clients in Fort Worth, Texas, the Bass Family, were major shareholders in Disney. Eventually, Disney hired the firm to design the Disney Vacation Club Clubhouse—a sales facility for Disney's timeshare offerings, the Disney Vacation Club. After schematic design, that project came to an abrupt halt when Disney cancelled the project for non-architectural reasons. However, the Schwarz team left a positive impression with Disney. When Disney embarked on the Disney Sports Complex—now known as ESPN's Wide World of Sports Complex—they returned to these architects for advice. Disney had already decided that their in-house design shop, the Imagineers, would be the design architects, and after a collegial discussion, Mr. Schwarz suggested they hire a sports architect as Architect of Record. Fast forward about another year, when three members of the architects' leadership were in Florida on other business, and the Disney Development Company invited them to Orlando. Disney had decided to replace the Imagineers. By the end of their meeting, Disney asked the architects to join an already in-progress project team meeting in a construction trailer a mile away.

ESPN's Wide World of Sports was planned as a collection of facilities to accommodate a wide range of amateur sports including tennis, baseball, softball, soccer, track and field events, cycling, gymnastics, and basketball, all situated in a park-like setting. To begin, the firm worked with the landscape architects to revise the master plan by incorporating a Main Street, an organizational concept common to most of Disney's parks. At the same time, Disney had been considering building a new theme park—a "fifth gate" for which this complex was thought to be the south anchor—and the Main Street could serve as the connector. The two featured structures are the ballpark and the fieldhouse. In addition to amateur games, the ballpark—designed to minor-league Triple-A standards—has been the spring training home for some Major League Baseball teams. The fieldhouse, depending upon its configuration, has up to eight basketball courts with minimal seating or a single center court with seating for 5,000 spectators. It was also used for the National Basketball Association's 2020 "Season in a Bubble." In addition to the two main structures, the firm designed several park structures throughout the landscape, including a tennis pavilion, other viewing facilities, and restrooms.

The Disney project team started with a predetermined aesthetic in mind for these buildings: red brick, like Fenway Park in Boston. In fact, they wrote that requirement into the Schwarz team's contract. So the architects completed schematic designs for red-brick buildings. During the presentation of those concepts to higher Disney executives, one asked Mr. Schwarz what he thought of the design. After a nod from Disney's team leader, Mr. Schwarz noted that Disney was expert at getting audiences to willingly suspend disbelief; however, even Disney was unlikely to get people to suspend disbelief to the point that they felt they were in New England in the middle of August in Orlando. When asked what the design direction should be, the architects suggested "Florida Picturesque," which they had used for the earlier, unexecuted Disney Vacation

Club Clubhouse design. Not really a historic style per se, Florida Picturesque is the firm's term for an eclectic mix of architectural elements as seen throughout Florida and based on its colonial, Spanish Mission heritage. The buildings are a rich cream-colored stucco with round-headed windows, bracketed cornices, sloped roofs, dark green metalwork, white accent trim, and balustrades. The ballpark and fieldhouse have arcades facing each other across a palm-lined pedestrian street.

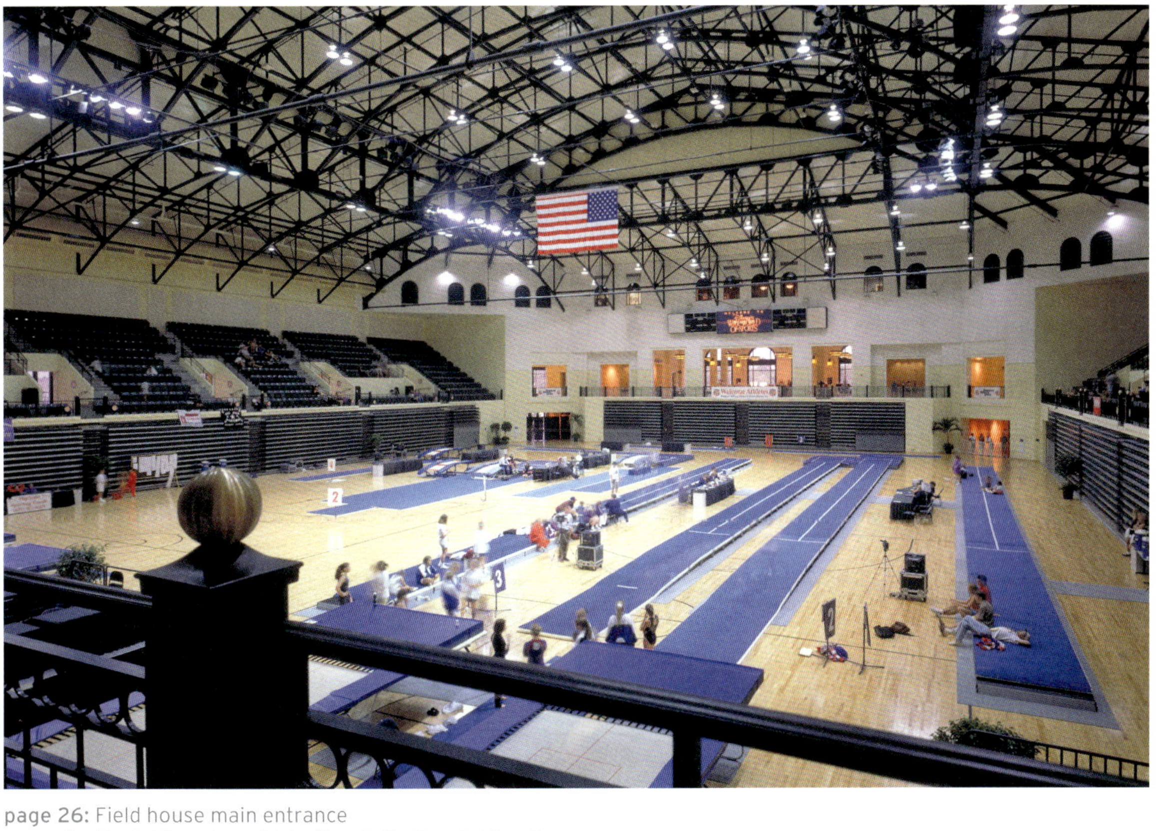

page 26: Field house main entrance
opposite (top): View down Main Street; **(bottom):** View from concourse
top: Ballpark
bottom: Field house, interior

AMERICAN AIRLINES CENTER

AMERICAN AIRLINES CENTER

Dallas, Texas, 2001
Client: Hillwood Development

As with The Ballpark in Arlington (see page 18), David M. Schwarz Architects won the commission for the American Airlines Center via a design competition, in this case a limited invitation to five prominent national firms. As the Schwarz team utilizes a highly client-interactive and iterative design process, design competitions usually place them at a distinct disadvantage. To overcome the disadvantage, they convinced the rather large and diverse client group to engage each firm in an interim design review prior to the due date for entries. This gave them an opportunity to present architecture as process, service, and more than just delivery of a product.

For the finals, the team presented numerous studies and options for all aspects of the building and grounds, including the master plan, iconic roof forms, concourse and seating-bowl arrangements, and exterior architectural styles. Because Ross Perot, Jr., majority owner of the Dallas Mavericks, owned 75 acres of developable land around the arena site—the Victory Park district that Dallas Stars principal owner, Thomas Hicks, would later buy into—the master plan was an unspoken criterion for landing the job. The Schwarz team noted that the civil engineers, retained before the competition, had designed a ten-lane arterial roadway to the east of the site, which would have effectively cut off the arena and Victory Park from the surrounding community. Instead, the architects suggested splitting the roadway into a more pedestrian-friendly pair of one-way streets, one on each side of the arena. That, along with their many façade options (to appeal to the client groups' wide-ranging tastes) and some pioneering interior circulation and bowl design concepts, proved victorious.

These innovative concepts were the most notable feature as the arena design advanced. Up until that date, most arenas had seating bowls surrounded by hippodrome-shaped, racetrack concourses with restrooms and concessions spread evenly around the perimeter. One only knew where one was by looking at the seating-section numbers on signage. Attendees had no inherent sense of where they were. Additionally, each seating level had its own concourse, often with no connections to the others. The firm was eager to break this mold. They did so by designing four grand lobbies—one at each end, and one on each side of the seating bowl. In these multistory lobbies, upper-level concourses became balconies overlooking the levels below. On their edges, these lobbies housed concessions and escalators. Large, semicircular windows provided views from each lobby at every level to different parts of the city, so that patrons would always know on what side of the arena they were. At the end of each lobby, the architects placed a circular turning point, which reoriented visitors by 45 degrees into smaller corner lobbies that provided access to restrooms and elevators. At each level, these turning spaces have circular floor openings, providing another opportunity to link the various levels. In each corner, the architects connected the suite levels and club-level concourse via modern glass and stainless-steel open stairways. Beyond the organizational and wayfinding benefits for the patron, this innovative approach had one substantial unique advantage: the teams were able to sell naming rights and sponsorship packages,

not only for the overall building and premium levels, but for each lobby as well. Each lobby sponsorship sold for as much as or more than some other arenas were getting for overall building naming rights. In its first decade and beyond, the Mavericks and Stars consistently led the NBA and NHL, respectively, in overall sponsorship income. The south lobby is the American Airlines Lobby where they displayed scale models of every aircraft the airline has flown.

On the exterior, the main features are the vaulted roof form, the above-mentioned semicircular windows into the lobbies, and the masonry bays and corner towers. A 350-foot-wide barrel vault spans the building side to side, east to west. Additional vaults, 250 feet wide, run north and south interacting with the main vault at four groins. The curved forms of the segmental vaults and semicircular windows relate to each other. The monumental roof form was a significant iconic element recognized from afar, and yet the firm consciously reduced the building's overall mass into human-scaled pieces, so that it was a friendly experience for pedestrians. The architects rendered the façades in a medium ironspot brick with accents of Indiana limestone, and a Swedish mahogany granite base. Window mullions are a light beige to match the limestone. On each façade, nearly 100-foot-high brick bays flank each side of the semicircular windows. Outboard of the bays, shorter yet broader towers mark the building's four corners. To the south, a plaza provides an outdoor event space and links the arena to the pedestrian-oriented Victory Park beyond. The plaza has a basin-less, flush-jet, programable fountain, which provides cooling and modulates the size of the plaza for various crowd sizes.

page 30: North entry arch
above: Plaza entry façade
right: N Houston Street entry façade

NORTH BOX O

AA
AA
AA
AMERICAN
AA
American Airlines
AA
AMERICAN
AA
American Airlines
AMERICAN AIRLINES CENTER
Sections 103-114
West & North Lobbies • South Box Office
FanShop
West Escalators to Upper Levels

opposite: South lobby
top left: Terrazzo and column detail
top right: Stair detail
below: Club-level seating

above: View from Club Restaurant
opposite: Arena floor set for hockey

JBL
DIRECTV
AMERICAN AIRLINES
American
UPS
FASTSIGNS
DIRECTV
Budweiser
Office DEPOT
RoomStore

DR PEPPER BALLPARK

Frisco, Texas, 2003
Client: Southwest Sports

Perhaps the most competitive part of Minor League Baseball is not the game on the field; rather it is municipalities competing against each other for the teams. Such was the case in Texas where Southwest Sports, then the new owners of the Texas Rangers, along with their partners Mandalay Entertainment, agreed to move the team's AA-affiliate from Louisiana to Frisco, Texas. The owners of the team, now dubbed the Frisco Rough Riders, turned to David M. Schwarz Architects to design the new ballpark in Frisco. The economics of the minor leagues require creative design solutions given the constraints of the business model: the host city pays the majority of the capital cost of the new facility, and the ownership pays for a limited number of "enhancements," such as an upgraded scoreboard. After the citizenry votes to approve the bond money, time is also of the essence. Thus the budget was tight and the schedule was incredibly fast. The Schwarz team understood that a traditional stadium design with a raised superstructure for the upper deck wasn't going to be possible given that the contractor could not procure the heavy, structural steel members within the budget or schedule. The suggested solution was to design several smaller, lightweight-steel-framed pavilions, arranged around the field in a park-like setting: a park within a park, so to speak.

The lower deck's structure could be poured-in-place concrete on grade, without structural steel supports. The smaller pavilions house concessions and restrooms on the lower level. Their upper levels are private suites with outdoor seating provided by projecting decks. Furthermore, these decks provide shade from the strong summer Texas sun for some of the lower-level seats. The design architects connected the upper levels with bridges to limit the number of vertical circulation cores. They accommodated the required cores in tower elements of a larger entrance structure behind home plate. This central building reads as the "clubhouse" for the other pavilions, not to be confused with the teams' clubhouses down the foul lines. On levels two through four, they placed a club restaurant, more suites, and the press box, respectively. The overall seating capacity is 10,200 fans with 8,700 in the main seating bowl and suites and 1,500 on the outfield grass. Attendance at the ballpark has been the highest in their league since 2005. For stylistic precedents, the firm looked at resort structures with a common reception and dining building. They fixed upon the wood-framed and wood-sided vernacular of Galveston, Texas's beachfront. The ballpark's clapboard-faced buildings are topped with sloped metal roofs, and the color palette of soft grays, creams, and beiges, all with off-white decorative trim, is also reminiscent of the Galveston precedents.

The park motif continues as the "concourse" on the outboard side of the pavilions, with informal landscaping featuring subtle topography, native plantings, and meandering crushed granite paths that lead to the batting cages and outfield seating on grassy slopes. Beyond the park, the architects provided Southwest Sports with a master plan for surrounding development, which included a hotel overlooking center field, and a multifamily residential and commercial development around the remaining perimeter. Beyond merely serving as the concourse for the ballpark, the "park" can be left open on non-game days to function as a park for the surrounding neighborhood. Likewise, some concession stands can operate on non-game days, so that neighborhood residents can have a grab-and-go lunch in the park.

page 38: View of home plate building from balcony suite
above (top): View of center field; **(bottom):** Main entrance

clockwise from top left: Course as an urban park;
On-grade concourse seen from balcony; Home plate building

ED SMITH STADIUM
HOME OF THE BALTIMORE ORIOLES
ORIOLES
HOME PLATE

ED SMITH STADIUM

Sarasota, Florida, 2011
Client: Sarasota County

The spring training and pre-season games of Major League Baseball provide a substantial economic engine for many Florida cities. Not only do local fans attend the games; fans from the major-league cities come down to see their favorite teams up close and personal, unlike the major-league experience at home. Therefore, these cities compete among themselves to land and retain the teams. After losing three teams in the twenty-year history of Ed Smith Stadium, the City of Sarasota offered a wide range of upgrades to and renovations of the dated facility in order to attract the Baltimore Orioles. This promise came with what some would consider an unreasonable schedule. While David M. Schwarz Architects initially felt the selection process and schedule might favor the original architects, both Sarasota's director of smart growth/urban planning and a representative of the Orioles strongly urged the firm to submit a response to the city's open Request for Proposals. After prevailing in the selection process, the architects were faced with the grueling schedule—early autumn until the winter holidays to complete their design—and the added criteria of designing renovations that a contractor could build within a commensurately tight schedule. Additionally, to not irritate their tax-paying citizens, the city set an equally tight project budget.

To satisfy the schedule and budget constraints, the firm decided to retain the existing structure of the seating bowl. They made only minimal changes to the seating to satisfy the barrier-free access requirements of the Americans with Disabilities Act and to improve sightlines behind the cross aisle. On the street side of the existing structure, they added what is effectively an architectural wrapper in front of the existing façades. The architects used the space within the width of this wrapper to improve the concourses, increase concessions, and add more up-to-date patron amenities.

Sarasota and its environs have two strong architectural heritages. In the downtown and surroundings, one finds excellent examples of what the firm calls "Florida Picturesque," an eclectic mix of materials and details that harken back to the state's Spanish Mission roots. The Ringling Family's Ca' d'Zan mansion (now the Ringling Museum) is a leading local example of this style. The other type of architecture, in and around the more residential areas, is known as the Sarasota School of midcentury modern, including a high school, residences, and other early works of the former dean of the Yale School of Architecture, Paul Rudolph. For the Ed Smith Stadium's new appearance, the architects selected the "Florida Picturesque" style.

The architects found that using this style's palette of materials was quite cost-effective. Simple fields of cream-colored stucco are ornamented with a judicious use of cast details for balconies, columns, window heads, and bracketed cornices. They used tile-work, another element of the style, in the Orioles' team colors, at select locations. At the street level, they employed a curving arcade of wide openings into the concourse. The length along two streets has been articulated with several different tower elements and second-level balconies overlooking the street. On the field side, this aesthetic was continued with stucco applied to the press box and other surfaces. It was not known if the existing roof structure could support

ED S
HOME OF THE
TICKETS

IUM
ORE ORIOLES

much additional load, so the architects used a fabric structure on a lightweight steel armature, which provides shade for the seating. The fabric will detach in strong winds and makes reference to the Ringling circus tents. Furthermore, the double-pointed split pennants that the design team used for various signage, inside and out, is more akin to circus pennants than traditional baseball pennants. For the renovation and expansion of the major-league players' clubhouse, the architects also utilized this picturesque style. A separate clubhouse for minor-league prospects is remotely located at Twin Lakes, where the architects employed the previously discussed Sarasota School of architecture.

page 42 and preceding: View from northwest
above (top): View along 12th Street concourse; **(bottom):** Main lobby
opposite: Landscape along street façade
following: View from visitors' bullpen

DICKIES ARENA

Fort Worth, Texas, 2019
Client: Event Facilities Fort Worth

For three weeks every late January and early February, the annual Fort Worth Stock Show and Rodeo (FWSSR) contributes significantly to the city's economy and cultural life. Economically, the event brings in thousands of ranchers, cowboys, cowgirls, spectators, and visitors to the livestock exhibits and the three daily rodeos. Culturally, Fort Worth prides itself as being the head of the historic Chisolm Trail, and thus "Where the West Begins."

The FWSSR is the United States' longest continually running livestock show and rodeo, having started in 1896. Since 1936, the Will Rogers Memorial Center has hosted the FWSSR within its 120-acre complex. The rodeo is performed in the center's coliseum. The coliseum, along with a matching auditorium, flank the Will Rogers Memorial's towering southwestern art deco spire, designed by noted architect Wyatt C. Hedrick. Although the event continued annually, by the turn of the twenty-first century the much-loved coliseum had become significantly outdated for both rodeo operations and patron amenity and comfort. Additionally, the coliseum could not be touched without bringing it up to current codes, which would have cost nearly as much as a new arena. Moreover, there was no ability for Fort Worth to bring in traveling shows and host other events, unless a bigger, more modern, and commodious arena was built. By the early 2000s, a public-private partnership between Event Facilities Fort Worth (EFFW) and the City of Fort Worth retained David M. Schwarz Architects to plan and design a state-of-the-art replacement. The project team selected a new site within the Will Rogers complex and design work began. However, the Great Recession of 2007–2009 brought planning to a halt after completion of the design development phase. The slow recovery meant the leaders would have to wait several years before they could mount a successful public-bond referendum to fund the city's part of the financial contribution. Finally, the referendum passed with 79 percent acceptance in November 2014, and design activities recommenced. Nevertheless, before construction of the arena could begin, a new 2,200-car garage—also designed by the firm—was required to replace surface parking, as many events would continue at the Will Rogers complex during construction. The city also used this period to complete roadway, parking-lot, and landscape improvements needed to support the new arena.

The nearly 750,000-square-foot Dickies Arena sits atop a 4-acre, landscaped plaza with commanding views of the Will Rogers campus and downtown Fort Worth. While it is a multipurpose facility—home to Texas Christian University (TCU) basketball, concerts, boxing, National Collegiate Athletic Association tournaments, hockey, family shows, and other events—the architects specifically designed unique features to support the rodeo. Below the plaza, a 156,000-square-foot livestock support building is at the arena's event level. This support level is fully conditioned and can be used as convention space for trade shows and similar events, thus making the arena capable of being used for an even larger range of events. The roof monitor for this level's equine warm-up ring becomes a pavilion in the plaza, providing natural light and spectator views to the ring below. Pipe and drape or

other moveable partitions can be used to convert the ring into a ballroom for even more flexibility. The architects also designed additional flexibility into the main event floor. Approximately two-thirds of the lower seating bowl utilizes articulating and moveable risers to provide optimum ring size for the rodeo, as well as excellent sightlines for basketball and hockey. The balance of the seating is on a club level and the upper bowl. The arena seats between 9,000 (rodeo) and 14,000 (center-stage concerts) patrons, depending on the event.

The architects designed the building to address people arriving from four distinct directions on the site so four unique entries and lobbies greet patrons on the cardinal points. The site is sloped from east to west so the arena is built on an 18-foot-high plinth. The roof of the plinth supports a 4-acre outdoor plaza, with three highly unique stairways encouraging patrons to enter the plaza from street level. On the exterior, the architects continued the design aesthetic of the historic campus in several ways. Two towers bookend the north entrance and pay homage to the original Will Rogers spire. The firm's brick, granite, and cast-stone choices were similar to and compatible with the landmark, although slightly darker in tone. Aluminum window walls and stainless-steel metalwork continue the southwestern art deco styling. And, as with most of these architects' public buildings, iconography is used to give the structure a sense of place. Four cast panels announce the arena's four primary uses: rodeo, sports, concerts, and family shows. The Will Rogers complex has a rich history of mosaics, starting with the initial Hedrick-designed buildings and continuing on subsequent exhibition structures and parking garages including, most recently, two mosaics incorporated into the façades of the arena garage. On Dickies Arena, the project team advanced the mosaic usage one step further by selecting artists to design two glass-tile mosaic murals. The one over the north entry between the towers, by Evergreene Architectural Arts (executed by Italian artisans), is a montage of multicultural Texas imagery and history; the one over the south entry at the bridge from the garage, by noted Western watercolorist William Matthews (executed by Mexican artisans), captures the movement of wild horses running among the Texas brush in an untamed landscape.

The architects carried both the art deco stylings and the use of iconography into Dickies' interiors. Inspiration for the interiors came from southwestern art deco, the culture surrounding the rodeo, and Texas flora. Texas prairie grasses and flowers, lassos, ropes, spurs, and stepped architectural geometries are incorporated into many of the building's surfaces and details, such as the terrazzo floors, carpets, railings, Western boot stitching in leather wall panels, stairways, and light fixtures. One beloved feature of the old coliseum was the exclusive Backstage Club. In the new Dickies Arena, the architects replaced the club with two multitiered clubs with wide-open views of both the event floor and lobbies below, one at each end of the club level. At the primary chute end of the arena, private boxes bracket the judges' platform and provide patrons with spectacular views of the animals entering the ring. The south club is an informal club with marche dining and two backlit onyx bars; the north club is the most exclusive gathering space in the facility with a fine-dining room.

page 50: North façade tower
above: View from the northwest
opposite: North façade with stairs
following: South façade with bridge

top left and bottom right: Octagonal staircase
bottom left and top right: Terrazzo detail
opposite: South lobby

top: Warm-up arena
bottom: Arena floor set for rodeo
opposite: Arena floor set for basketball

Dickies Arena
TEXAS
4 T.O.L.
4 FOULS
11
11:36
1ST HALF
5
TEXAS A&M

OFFICE & RESIDENTIAL

1718

1718 CONNECTICUT AVENUE NW

Washington, D.C., 1979
Client: Property Company of America

The building at 1718 Connecticut Avenue, NW in Washington, D.C.'s Dupont Circle Historic District, holds a special place, near and dear, to the hearts of long-term colleagues at David M. Schwarz Architects. It was the firm's first new-construction, concrete-frame elevator building after years of designing decks, additions, townhouse renovations, and commercial historic restorations.

The opportunity to land this commission grew out of their design work for the restoration and expansion of 1722 and 1724 Connecticut Avenue NW, immediately to the north. The client group for these renovations were partners in a prestigious Washington law firm. One member was pro bono counsel for what is now the DC Preservation League. In that capacity, he wrote the newly enacted D.C. historic preservation law. As these projects were nearing completion of construction, the zoning commission began considering a major downzoning for the historic district. If the new zoning was approved, one would not be able to construct buildings as large as the renovated historic structure on the parking lot to the south. The same client group owned the parking lot. In order to grandfather their development rights, they had one instruction for the Schwarz firm: "Design a building that would be approved by the Joint Committee on Landmarks (now Historic Preservation Review Board) on its first presentation and could financially cover its debt service the day it was complete."

Having carefully studied the neighborhood characteristics while working on the lots next door, the firm was well suited for this assignment. They had also worked with neighborhood groups and the city's preservation office in achieving the necessary approval for the prior project. The keys to approval were to gain citizens' support by preserving the sense of streetscape, and to remove the additional density from that streetscape. The building's massing was crafted to align the eave line with the building to the north's ridge line, and to align the building's cornice line with the cornice line of the building to the south. After that, the architects set back the top two floors far enough that these were not visible from the sidewalk on that side of the street. Lastly, they shaped additional height, needed for mechanical equipment and an elevator machine room, as Victorian-inspired tower elements, one with a clock. Neighbors affectionately called it "the cuckoo clock building." The architects continued to work with the local citizens' association and the city's preservation office, and indeed the building was approved during the first public hearing; it was the only building to do so for the next ten years.

The building was designed during the height of the postmodern movement in American architecture; however, the firm does not consider 1718 to be postmodern. The design incorporates elements from throughout the historic district such as bays, round-headed windows, cornices, corbelled brickwork, and the like. However, each of these elements is appropriately scaled and used as they would have been historically. No exaggerated mannerism was used. Similarly, they used material prevalent nearby in traditional ways: rich, red bricks, grapevine-tooled mortar joints, contrasting accent bricks, slate shingles, and limestone details. Beyond the immediate context,

page 62 and above: Connecticut Avenue façade
opposite (left): Setback terrace on sixth floor; **(right):** Rear façade

the architects looked to the works of past architects for design inspiration including H. H. Richardson's Trinity Church in Boston and several of Frank Furness's buildings in Philadelphia. This liberal quotation of various historic styles is an early example of what the Schwarz team now refers to as its neo-eclectic style.

Again, the clients necessitated that the project be financially viable. While the detailed and ornamented masonry façades were not inexpensive compared to some more modern intrusions in the district built not long before the preservation law, the firm offset these costs by quoting a far less expensive style for parts of the side façades and the alley façade, which are not visible from the streetscape. This was the International Style of early modernism, executed in Portland cement stucco on concrete block. An efficient floor plan and curb appeal, which led to a short lease-up period, both further contributed to the building's economy. While the client groups' original intention was merely to vest their property rights, they sold the project at a significant profit to the Washington office of a major national office developer. Construction commenced a day before the permit would have expired, and the vesting of the building rights would have expired along with the permit.

1133
1133

1133 CONNECTICUT AVENUE NW

Washington, D.C., 1989
Client: The Lenkin Company

David M. Schwarz Architects' involvement with 1133 Connecticut Avenue in Washington, D.C. had a very unusual beginning. Mr. Schwarz was visiting the offices of The Lenkin Company—the client for two of the firm's prior designs—to discuss a different potential project, when another architect's model for the commercial building at 1133 Connecticut Avenue arrived. Mr. Lenkin asked Mr. Schwarz what he thought of it. He said that his mother, like most mothers, had taught him that if he didn't have something nice to say, not to say anything at all. Mr. Lenkin then asked if the Schwarz firm could do better, evoking the reply, "After saying that, we better be able to do better." The exchange continued with, "Okay, you have two weeks." As the current design was nearing completion of contract documents, construction was about to start, and the city had already issued a building permit, the ground rules were set such that they could not change the concrete-framed structure, save for an allowance to shift exterior columns no more than a short distance.

Returning in two weeks with a rough study model, elevations, and a rendering, the firm received Mr. Lenkin's agreement that their assertion was correct and, in fact, they could do better. Their new design was based on the Louis Sullivan analogy that a building, like a column, must have a base, shaft, and capital. In this case, the base is the first three stories, clad in Indiana limestone with stylized classical detailing. This reads as a ground floor with mezzanine (actually, the second floor) and an attic story (actually, the third floor). The limestone base sits on a Canadian green granite plinth and has a limestone balustrade on top. The shaft consists of seven additional floors of offices, and the capital is the final two floors of offices, with similar detailing to the base, rendered in architectural precast concrete to match the limestone below. The architects were not satisfied merely with this vertical separation; they wanted differentiation along the shaft's perimeter as well. Their design utilizes tower-like elements separating three areas of glass curtainwall. The architects curved the middle section of curtainwall at the corner to pay homage to the landmark Mayflower Hotel across DeSales Street. They further divided these towers into outer beige brick bays and inner precast window frames and spandrel panels. Although one normally considers curtainwall a modern material, the architects wanted a transitional read to relate to the more classically inspired masonry and precast. They settled on a syncopated rhythm of major and minor mullions in both the horizontal and vertical directions. The green, minor members are standard aluminum pieces, and the major members are break-formed sheet copper, the appearance of which changes over time as a patina slowly develops. Lastly, between the towers, the firm added limestone "temple" elements, which rise into the curtainwall at the fourth and fifth floors.

The firm worked with the original architect to rapidly incorporate the changes into the contract documents. During this time, the client kept increasing the Schwarz team's design scope. First came the main lobby and ground-floor elevator lobby, then the elevator cabs, and finally the standard upper-floor lobbies and restrooms. Each new assignment came with its own set of constraints and restrictions. Of very real interest was the economic

affect that these changes had on the pro forma. Because the developer had bid the prior plans with the trades, he knew the exact cost of the aesthetic improvements. Mr. Lenkin was also completing another office building across Connecticut Avenue when construction on 1133 began. Location, location, location, as the saying goes, was not a factor. The building at 1133 was fully leased before the earlier building and rented for significantly higher rates, thus proving the firm's long-espoused maxim: "Good architecture pays!" The improved architecture more than paid for itself. In addition, because of good relations with the client and the interrelationships between the development community, financial community, and the firm, these architects had the unique opportunity to design three different office suites for investment companies in the same part of the building on three different floors. These spanned the decades from 1990 to 2019, using some similar features yet vastly different stylistic approaches and materials.

page 66: Entrance from Connecticut Avenue
opposite (top): Common space in a contemporary office suite;
(bottom): Offices in a custom-paneled office suite
above: Corner view

1201 F STREET NW

Washington, D.C., 1990
Client: Carr America Realty Corporation

The realization of 1201 F Street, NW in Washington, D.C.'s Downtown Historic District took two decades. In the early 1980s, David M. Schwarz Architects was approached by a consortium of landholders to design an office building for the northwest corner of 12th and F Streets, across from a Metro Center subway entrance. The District of Columbia was about to change the downtown parking requirement in its zoning regulations, and the property owners wanted to vest their rights under the old zoning. They thought underground parking, within a few yards of the below-grade Metro Center station, would be unfeasible and/or financially prohibitive. After the architects advanced design and documentation to a degree that they could file a placeholder drawing set with the building department, the clients put a hold on the project. They had no intention of building anytime soon; they just wanted to vest the zoning.

Several years later, after the clients changed the lead developer and acquired two more adjacent lots—including the venerable Reeve's Bakery, home of the famous blueberry doughnuts and fried chicken—they returned to the firm for a new design of a larger building. Nevertheless, the new commission came with severe time constraints. The developer was trying to hit a specific rental-market opening for the building's completion. Although people previously thought the presence of the federal government made Washington recession-proof, after the team had completed 90 percent of construction documents, a steep, sooner-than-expected recession hit the district's real-estate sector at the end of the decade. The clients halted the project once again. Even as the economy recovered, the client group was unwilling to start construction without a significant lead tenant. Every couple of years, they would ask the architects to dust off the plans and make minor revisions, before presenting them to a prospective tenant. Events proceeded in this manner until the late 1990s, when the developer bought out their partners and decided to build the building on speculation. Again, they asked for additional changes before commencing construction.

The overall architectural read of this twelve-story structure is one of neo-secessionism, a style the firm employed because of its transitional nature, neither classical nor cutting-edge modern, appropriate for both the historic district and the target rental market segment. Originally designed as an all-limestone building, its materiality was one of the client-mandated changes. The designers retained a two-story, Indiana limestone base. Of note, in an agreement with the property owner to the west, which allowed the building to have additional height and area under a peculiarity in the district's zoning regulation, the clients agreed to set back the western face 20 feet from the adjacent structure, above the second floor. Rather than simply extruding the building's base horizontally by another structural bay, the architects decided to treat this condition as if it were an outparcel by designing a separate and more detailed standalone limestone façade. Above the second floor, the building is beige brick with architectural precast panels at the middle of its projecting bays. The top two levels are all architectural precast to match the limestone base,

including the structural trellises. Another change was the building's top, considered an unoccupied, architectural embellishment by the code. Shallow bays on each side are joined into tower elements by these stepping, square embellishments; they were previously designed as stepping, concentric circular forms. Yet another change was the client's insistence on corner windows for the corner offices, an aesthetic not consistent with the balance of the building's design. To accommodate their client's mandate, the architects reintroduced a curvilinear form. Alternating quarter-round windows and spandrel panels connect the adjacent bays, and are topped with a copper quarter dome, at the eleventh floor. This was perhaps the firm's earliest use of curves at their building's corners, a motif they would return to often over the next two decades.

The final requested change was the lobby. On the side of caution, the developer had the architects swap the neo-secessionism design for a more traditional, albeit a tad staid, marble and wood design in shades of brown and beige. The project's long-awaited completion came with two ironies. First, the developer landed a prestigious New York law firm, which was opening a Washington office, as the lead tenant shortly after breaking ground on a speculative basis. The rest of the floors rented soon thereafter. Second, while the original owners were afraid of the pending new parking requirement, the building has four levels of below-grade parking.

page 70: Corner at F Street and 12th Street NW
above: Aerial view showing stepped massing
opposite: Lobby

1201 F
STREET

THE SARATOGA

Washington, D.C., 1986
Client: Horning Brothers

The site of the Saratoga apartment building on Connecticut Avenue—one of Washington, D.C.'s premiere apartment-building boulevards—had been in the developer's family since they built the Chesapeake next door during the Great Depression. The site had remained vacant ground for over half a century. As such, the Forest Hills neighbors to the east considered it part of the adjacent Forest Hills Park and Playground. On the other hand, the developer wished to maximize gross floor area via the Planned Unit Development (PUD) process, which requires D.C. Zoning Commission approval. However, D.C. laws gives Advisory Neighborhood Commissions (ANCs) "great weight" in all community matters before the commission, posing a dilemma in this not-in-my-backyard locality. The solution: the developer hired David M. Schwarz Architects, known for their ability to get maximum density projects approved in historic districts and other neighborhoods skeptical of new development.

The PUD regulations required that such new developments provide significant community benefit in exchange for relief from strict zoning requirements. For the Saratoga, among the benefits was exceptional architecture. The architects carefully studied and borrowed liberally from the "great addresses" that lined upper Connecticut Avenue. Fortunately, or unfortunately depending upon one's point of view, the immediate context featured several 1950s through 1970s apartment houses, lacking in the curb appeal and architectural detail of their earlier neighbors. This provided the opening for ultimate and timely approval of the Schwarz design. The architects paid tribute to the grander local precedents, provided ample detail at key locations, and created a human scale lacking in much of the immediate context. By presenting designs on several occasions to the ANC and the civic association, the team entered all public hearings with full community support. Thus, the Saratoga became the first non-subsidized, built-for-rental apartment building constructed in the District of Columbia since the 1968 riots.

The Saratoga is a modified-H in plan. Unequal legs, projecting to the west, form an entry court and help comfortably resolve the clash between Washington's street grid and its diagonal avenues. While the building's deference to the best of the Connecticut Avenue examples produced a design, which at first glance reads more traditional than not, the Saratoga does not directly copy any past historical style. In fact, it is actually very much of its own time. On the interior, many units are oriented on a diagonal to maximize long-range views up and down the avenue and over Forest Hills to Rock Creek Park beyond. These units project beyond the main building plane with bays that extend the units. Along with inset balconies, behind the building plane, much of that plane becomes merely a brick screen-wall with projecting and receding building elements. Such an overall architectural read would have been quite peculiar on any of its historic precedents.

THE SARATOGA
4·6·0·1

"Special praise should be sung for the fact that the building is fully designed in the round—what's true of the street-facing façades applies equally to the rear façades, which in characteristic Washington fashion encompass a nice private garden."

—Benjamin Forgey

page 74: Corner façade and neighboring context along Connecticut Avenue NW
left: Gardens and entry
following: Façade along Saratoga Street NW

THE
SARATOGA

2700

THE WOODLEY

Washington, D.C., 2014
Client: The JBG Companies

In 1918, Harry Wardman, a noted Washington, D.C. apartment-building developer, decided to venture into the hospitality market with the construction of the Wardman Park Hotel on Connecticut Avenue. This hotel, modeled after the Homestead resort in Virginia's Blue Ridge Mountains, was the largest in the city at the time, but was quickly nicknamed "*Wardman's Folly*," as it was north of Rock Creek and far from the developed city. However, it proved phenomenally successful. Although the historic building was retained in 1980, a modern replacement opened on the site, and in 2005 the property was purchased by prominent D.C.-area developers, the JBG Companies (now JBG Smith). Thereafter, they planned a new condominium on the property, utilizing unbuilt gross square footage allowable under the zoning code. This was the highest piece of large unbuilt ground in the city with potential for remarkable views. Then came the 2007–2009 Great Recession. After the recovery, the JBG Companies decided to change the project to high-end rental apartments. A test marketing study revealed substantial concerns with the marketability of the original architect's design. The developers requested major changes, but the architect showed little appetite for making them. The JBG Companies then asked three other firms to submit their best ideas for modifying the project: one firm from Chicago, one from nearby Alexandria, Virginia, and David M. Schwarz Architects. Depending upon one's perspective, one could say they all won. The Schwarz firm was hired for the exteriors, the Chicago firm for the interiors, and the Alexandria firm as Architect of Record.

The JBG Companies already had a building permit for the project, so they were going to submit the revised plans as a permit revision, which was somewhat of a stretch. The new design had to have exactly the same gross floor area, and the massing had to be reasonably close to the previous design. Ultimately, the only thing the new design had in common with the old design was the modified U-shaped plan. The original Wardman Park Tower, still on the same property, served as the design inspiration for the new architects. The firm employed similar brick; cast stone to match limestone; curved, inflecting balconies; oval accent windows; multiple bays; and neo-Edwardian details. Taking full advantage of the views, the architects developed a multilevel roof deck experience in conjunction with the noted landscape architecture firm Michael Vergason Landscape Architects.

During design, the JBG Companies had second thoughts about the Chicago firm's plans for the ground-floor amenities, and they shifted this scope to the Schwarz team. Everyone agreed on a progression of variously scaled spaces (entry lobbies, reception, crossing square, living room, and library), all quite traditional and entirely compatible with both the exterior design and target market. Materials and features included patterned marble floors, wood paneling, and coffered and vaulted ceilings. The architects also selected the furniture. The sequence of spaces created a through-lobby with the rear overlooking a Vergason-designed linear water feature with an infinity-edge, which cascades to the swimming pool on a lower terrace.

A few months after completion, the JBG Companies sold the Woodley to an investor group for $50 million dollars over pro forma—once again proving the David M. Schwarz Architects maxim: "Good architecture pays."

"The Woodley is the first luxury high-rise apartment building to be built in decades in Woodley Park, one of the District's most prestigious and historic residential neighborhoods, and it will redefine the standard for luxury apartment homes in the D.C. market."

—Dave Nachison
Senior Managing Director, HFF Realty

page 80: Garden façade detail
preceding: Entry court
above and right: Rooftop trellis and gardens
opposite: Garden façade

opposite: Garden lobby with painted paneling
top: Vestibule between garden and entry lobby
bottom: View from entry through building

top: Club room
bottom: Library
opposite: Library alcove

HAVANA
LECNIK
OSCAR NIEMEYER
HOUSES

OPEN 24 HOURS
RITE AID PHARMACY
OPEN 24 HOURS
RITE AID
RITE AID

13|U

Washington, D.C., 2017
Client: The JBG Companies

The 13|U building at the southwest corner of 13th and U Streets in the Northwest quadrant of Washington, D.C. is one of more than a dozen projects that David M. Schwarz Architects has designed for prominent local developers, the JBG Companies—now JBG Smith. Set in a rapidly changing neighborhood—once riot-scarred—13|U now possesses some of Washington's most valuable real estate. However, the prior building on the site was a one-story retail structure erected in the early 1990s. The program and corresponding design went through several iterations. Starting in 2007, it was first planned as a boutique hotel, garnering some support from the Cardozo/Shaw neighborhood, albeit some community members were concerned about the design's 115 feet of height. During the financial crisis that began at the end of that year, JBG decided to proceed slowly, though they had the architects look at a program adjustment with a smaller hotel, coupled with condominium apartments with hotel services. During this period, the firm also studied what to do about one existing retail tenant—a national chain pharmacy that had a thirty-year lease with much of the term remaining. With the tenant not inclined to leave, the architects and developer worked through many scenarios to keep them on the site or build around them. Finally, the drugstore agreed to temporarily move its prescriptions business (its most profitable department) and some limited merchandise into trailers, which would be placed along the deep setback adjacent to the 13th Street sidewalk. Eventually, the client changed the program to an all-rental apartment building in 2011.

At the start of design, the architects presented their clients with four concepts, and because a change in zoning was required to achieve increased height and allowable gross square footage for the building, they all agreed upon the scheme with the strongest relationship to the historic district. The basic concept remained intact throughout the programmatic changes; although, given concerns expressed by D.C.'s Office of Planning and the Historic Preservation Office, the architects lowered the height to 90 feet. Community support increased, save for the owners of the townhouses across the alley to the south. The firm met with them several times and moved some density further away on the site. In the end, the project received the support of the local Advisory Neighborhood Commission, along with necessary approvals from the Zoning Commission and Historic Preservation Review Board.

Massing-wise, the architects divided the U Street façade into seven parts with end pavilions, hyphens (with rounded balconies inflecting across the hyphen to each other), and a central entry piece comprising outer rectangular bays and a segmental-curved central oriel. The oriel rests upon a balcony, supported by decorative brackets, which acts as a canopy for the recessed entrance. With each of these elements either projecting toward or setting back from U Street, as one walks down the sidewalk, one never sees the building's whole mass at the same time, making its mass far more compatible with the historic district. This is a strikingly refreshing counterpoint to most of the new intrusions into the neighborhood. The 13th Street façade has a center mass,

bordered by broad, curved corners sweeping toward U Street and the alley. The architects stepped back upper floors along both streets and the alley to further modulate the overall form. The top of the alley façade, above the height of the Wallach Place townhouses, is quite visible from the south, so the architects placed as much time and care in its design as they did with the street façades. Materials are predominately a medium red, wide-range, ironspot brick and beige, limestone-like cast stone. The stone is concentrated at the base, with a trellised top floor of central mass, center element of the end pavilions, and accents at window heads and sills. A cast stone cartouche above the entry has two opposing saxophones, an iconograph reference to the U Street Corridor's past as the center of Washington's once-thriving jazz scene.

Upon completion, 13|U has achieved among the highest rents per square foot of anywhere in the city, yet another example by the firm that good architecture pays.

page 90: U Street entrance
top (from left to right): Curved bay at entry; Detail of west belvedere; Terrace within belvederes
right: View from Wallach Place NW and 13th Street NW
opposite: Stainless-steel entry doors
following: View from corner of 13th Street NW and U Street NW

1310

OPEN 24
HOURS
RITE AID
PHARMACY
RITE
AID

STORAGE
ELLINGTO

THE WAYCROFT

Arlington, Virginia, 2020
Client: The B.F. Saul Companies and Afilliates

The site of the Waycroft was a former car dealership at the 100-percent-corner of the Ballston mixed-use neighborhood in Arlington, Texas. The site was purchased by Saul Centers, a multigenerational legacy builder, which historically develops for long-term ownership. For the project, they decided to hold a mini-competition among three invited firms including David M. Schwarz Architects, who had met with them a few years earlier. The site sat at the transition between Ballston's eleven- to fourteen-story high-rises in the central business district and the two- to three-story Bluemont residential neighborhood to the west. For the competition, the firm submitted two designs: one was a by-right development under existing zoning, with some variation in height, and the other stacked more height and density at the corner of Wilson Boulevard and Glebe Road and reduced height and density at Tazewell Street and 7th Street. Saul Centers hired the firm and selected the taller option.

This would be the architect's first experience with Arlington County's site-plan approval process, known as a 4.1 submission. The client's project manager warned the architects that it would not be a pleasant or easy experience. The schematic design closely followed the selected competition entry, breaking the full-block project into four or five connected buildings, with the taller, 130-foot-high pieces facing the Ballston central business district and lower buildings opposite the adjacent residential neighborhood. Then the fun began: seven meetings with citizen members of the Site Plan Review Committee, each meeting with its own subject focus. As major retail developers, Saul Centers wanted a space for an urban grocery store. Arlington had a prohibition against curb cuts on Wilson Boulevard or Glebe Road for loading or parking access, thus the architects had to locate these on the side streets. Consequently, circulation, traffic, and parking became the greatest sticking points with the community. The architects made reasonable adjustments to satisfy their concerns. Interestingly, when it came to the meeting on architectural design, for the most part the community was well receptive of the design, including the increased height, and there was little major opposition. Only one citizen concern remained: they were not used to full-block buildings of this scale in Ballston. Splitting the block in two would have destroyed the grocery-store location and bifurcated the apartments. To address the issue, the firm provided a 30-foot-wide gap between the two main façades facing Glebe Road—a kind of faux alley break—that extended back only as far as the apartment-building corridor, thus still allowing the apartment component to operate as one building. At the end of the 4.1 process, the project received what the firm refers to as the closest 5–0 vote ever, in that two or three of the council members had said they would vote against the project from the outset.

Saul Centers' leadership had a fondness for the art deco style. Their ancestor, a banker, had issued the construction loan for Washington's historic Kennedy-Warren Apartments, and when the project suffered from the Great Depression, the family foreclosed and finished the project. Saul Centers still owns that property today. The architects used that landmark as design inspiration for the tallest and most prominent portion of the project, even

selecting similar brick and other materials. Along Tazewell Street, they designed what appears from the streetscape to be four-story, urban, low-rise apartment buildings, which actually have a setback fifth floor. From the street, they screened the view of the taller structure beyond. The rest of the project required significantly more study. The architects explored art moderne and even more modern solutions for the corner of 7th Street and Glebe Road, but the client was never comfortable with that direction. In reviewing mortar colors with the client, a field trip to the Woodley (see page 80) provided the necessary, yet unexpected inspiration for that building's redesign, which all happened quickly amid the public review process.

The architects also designed the project interiors, including apartment plans and finishes, lobbies, public circulation spaces, and resident amenity areas. Each of the three primary buildings has its own entry lobby, yet for operational reasons, Saul Centers wanted all the corridors to connect into a single building. However, to maintain the sense of each building's individuality, the architects arranged corridors and elevator lobbies with off-sets in the circulation path, which avoided any racetrack effect. Stylistically, the interiors match the aesthetics of their associated exterior façades, with variation between them, regarding materials, stone and wood varieties, cabinetry, flooring, trim profiles, and the like. However, the different color schemes are interrelated, sharing certain base colors between them. Even during a year of COVID-19 pandemic restrictions, in the first ten months of occupancy, tenants rented over 80 percent of the 491 units, far outpacing both its competitors in the Arlington market and the client's pro forma.

page 96: Crown detail at the intersection of Glebe Road and Wilson Boulevard
above: Building at the Corner of Wilson Street and Glebe Road with context
opposite (clockwise from top): Second aesthetic expression at Glebe Road and 7th Street North; View along Tazewell Street; Inner courtyard showing the intersection of the various architectural expressions
following: Interior courtyard

preceding (left): Sidewalk retail along Glebe Road; **(right):** One of the building's three lobbies
clockwise from top: The art deco-inspired lobby at the corner of Glebe Road and Wilson Boulevard; Stair detail; Elevators off the lobby
opposite: Mahogany-paneled club room

MIXED-USE, RETAIL, & HOSPITALITY

BERINGER WINE ESTATES

St. Helena, California, 2001
Client: Beringer Vineyards

David M. Schwarz Architects has had the good fortune to have had one of its earliest and most loyal clients form a highly successful private equity firm, the Texas Pacific Group. TPG, as it is known, has acquired many well-known and prestigious portfolio companies, including Beringer Wine Estates, then the owners of Beringer, Chateau St. Jean and Stags' Leap wineries. While the TPG portfolio companies sometimes became business prospects for the architects, TPG never imposed the firm on their acquisitions: the architects had to sell their value to the company's management. With Beringer, this was a somewhat tricky situation. The California wine industry is a unique mix of highly sophisticated brand managers and unpretentious grape farmers. It was the branding side that provided the Schwarz firm with their opening. Visiting the wineries on a very hot summer day, they realized how underwhelming the visitor experience was. Walking through parking lots, waiting in long lines, lack of shade, crowded tasting rooms, and having to lug cases of wine all the way back to the parking lot were not ways to build brand loyalty.

In the wine business, this aspect of the business is known as hospitality, further defined as two types: trade hospitality (for critics, distributors, restauranters, and the like) versus consumer hospitality. While direct retail sales at the winery account for a very small portion of overall sales, the major benefit of consumer hospitality is to build that aforementioned brand loyalty. The key is not how many bottles or cases the customer buys there; it is getting them to buy more of your wines at their neighborhood wine shop or supermarket. Eventually, Beringer hired the Schwarz team to re-envision their consumer hospitality experience.

At the Beringer winery in the St. Helena district of Napa Valley, planning began by relocating the parking away from the historic mid-1880s Rhine House, and interspersing shade trees among the new parking. Then the team designed a new carriage entry pavilion—featuring natural stone and reclaimed redwood—that provided for orientation and ticketing on the way in, and case pickup (proximate to parking) on the way out. Up the hill, the architects converted the underutilized old winery into exhibit space, retail sales, and a new tasting for the large number of visitors. As a protected historic structure, all changes required approval of the California State Historic Preservation Office. Furthermore, the building had to meet current seismic and energy codes, not an easy undertaking for a structure more than a century old. For casework, furniture, and finishes in the new facilities and site furnishing on the grounds, the architects reused redwood, reclaimed from giant wood casks no longer used for wine production. Other site work included new and revamped plantings, and the path from the Gatehouse to the Old Winery features a grape "petting zoo" exhibiting the varietals grown in the vineyards. Of additional importance, the relocation of the main tasting room out of the Rhine House allowed this historic resource to be renovated and limited to more private tastings of the reserve wines and other higher-end offerings.

At Chateau St. Jean, across the mountains in Sonoma Valley, the original château was subjected to similar

overuse as the Rhine House was at the Beringer winery. Adding a new tasting room and retail sales building was paramount in the hospitality program; however, as with the winery at Beringer, revamping the visitor experience began with the parking. The design team relocated some existing parking to make room for a bilaterally symmetrical, formal garden and the required new structure. The garden reorients arriving patrons toward the new tasting and retail structure. The architects located this structure parallel to and approximately 60 feet from the château, creating a more enclosed entry garden serving both buildings. Other new gardens provide outdoor seating. Throughout, trees, umbrellas, and trellises provide relief from the hot California sun. The architects envisioned the new building as an orangery within these gardens. It is a pale beige stucco edifice with a hipped, red-tile roof and Mediterranean details, both compatible with and deferential to the historic château building. All fenestrations are multilight French doors topped with semi-circular transoms. The interior features open, wooded, flat-top, king post trusses and wood planks at the ceiling and French limestone tiles on the floor. An expansive wooden bar, topped with a zinc counter and a glass-fronted back bar, handle the tasting duties, and custom wood casework and central farm tables handle the food and retail offerings. With the bulk of the tasting and retail moved into this new facility, the château's use is now limited to reserve tastings.

At both properties path and place were a key component of enhancing the visitor experience. In other words, the restoration or addition of useable outdoor gardens, along with improvements to existing and the addition of new walkways, which connect the gardens to each other and the buildings, have all transformed the landscape. The architects worked with the award-winning landscape architecture firm Olin Partnership in the layout of these features and plant selections. In their joint effort, they maximized the benefits of Napa Valley's unique climate. Napa County has more native plant species than any other county in the United States—with Sonoma not far behind—giving the designers a wide variety of plants from which to pick.

page 108: Repurposed old winery
above: Order pickup desk
opposite (top): Orientation pavilion at Beringer winery; **(bottom):** Welcome desk at Beringer winery

A NAPA VALLEY ESTATE
ESTABLISHED 1876
TODAYS OFFERINGS
UPCOMING EVENTS
WELCOME TO
BERINGER VINEYARDS
HISTORIC TOUR TIMES

opposite: View from pavilion to historic winery
top: Gardens at historic winery
bottom: Repurposed old winery

left: Historic Chateau St. Jean
above: Tasting pavilion

SUNDANCE SQUARE MASTER PLANNING AND BUILDINGS

Fort Worth Texas, 1988–2014
Client: Sundance Square Management

When David M. Schwarz Architects first started working in Fort Worth, Texas, most of downtown, especially its north end, was close to an unsafe, unwalkable, unlivable, underutilized, urban tragedy. As in many downtowns in American cities, large and small, post–World War II government policies and the rapid expansion of automobile ownership led to a large population exodus to the suburbs. This prompted many city leaders to embrace an ill-conceived, futuristic, unrealistic urban redevelopment scheme, which was more urban removal than urban renewal. What followed was massive demolition without any redevelopment. The one bright spot was the Bass family's developments in the early to mid-1980s: two high-rise office towers, the renovation of two square blocks of historic, low-rise structures, and a two-block hotel and conference center in an area that once served as the hideout of Butch Cassidy and the Sundance Kid. Sundance Square was rising once again. Otherwise, as Mr. Schwarz would say, "You could shoot a cannon down Main Street at 5:00 pm and not hit anyone."

The Bass family had acquired significantly more land than they had utilized for these initial projects. After the firm assisted one family member in halting a nearby overhead highway expansion, another family member retained the firm to create a master plan for their holdings, which needed to be coherent and economically feasible, as well as one that could be phased over time. The goal was a mixed-use, vibrant, enjoyable, livable, twenty-four-hour neighborhood worthy of Fort Worth's rich history as "Where the West Begins." The firm's initial analysis showed myriad challenges: far too many surface parking lots and unbuilt parcels, far too many vacant buildings, too many impediments to pedestrian travel, and perhaps most importantly, not a single block where all four sides presented a safe and pleasant walking experience. To correct this would require improving both sides of the street around one block. After the firm presented their findings, the client group responded, "Texans don't walk." In response, Mr. Schwarz stated that no one had given Texans nice places to walk, so it was no surprise that they didn't.

The ambitions set out in the plan were incremental, starting one block at a time to provide the ability to perambulate one block, and then move on to the next; and then to build on the strengths of the restored building and continue to add a variety of uses. The first project was Sundance West, an eleven-story brick building that steps down to the heights of the historic building to the east. This mixed-use project contained rental apartments, ground-floor retail, a vastly successful cineplex, and a custom penthouse apartment. The units were the first in downtown Fort Worth since World War II. Next followed Sundance East, another mixed-use project a few blocks to the east. This one included more movie screens, expanded retail and dining offerings, and offices above. The architects used one of their signature design devices, breaking down this full block structure into separate smaller-scale façades respectful of their context. Sundance Square became lively into the evening. Cultural and civic development followed with Bass Hall (see page 256), the Maddox Muse Center, and the renovation and expansion of the Central Library.

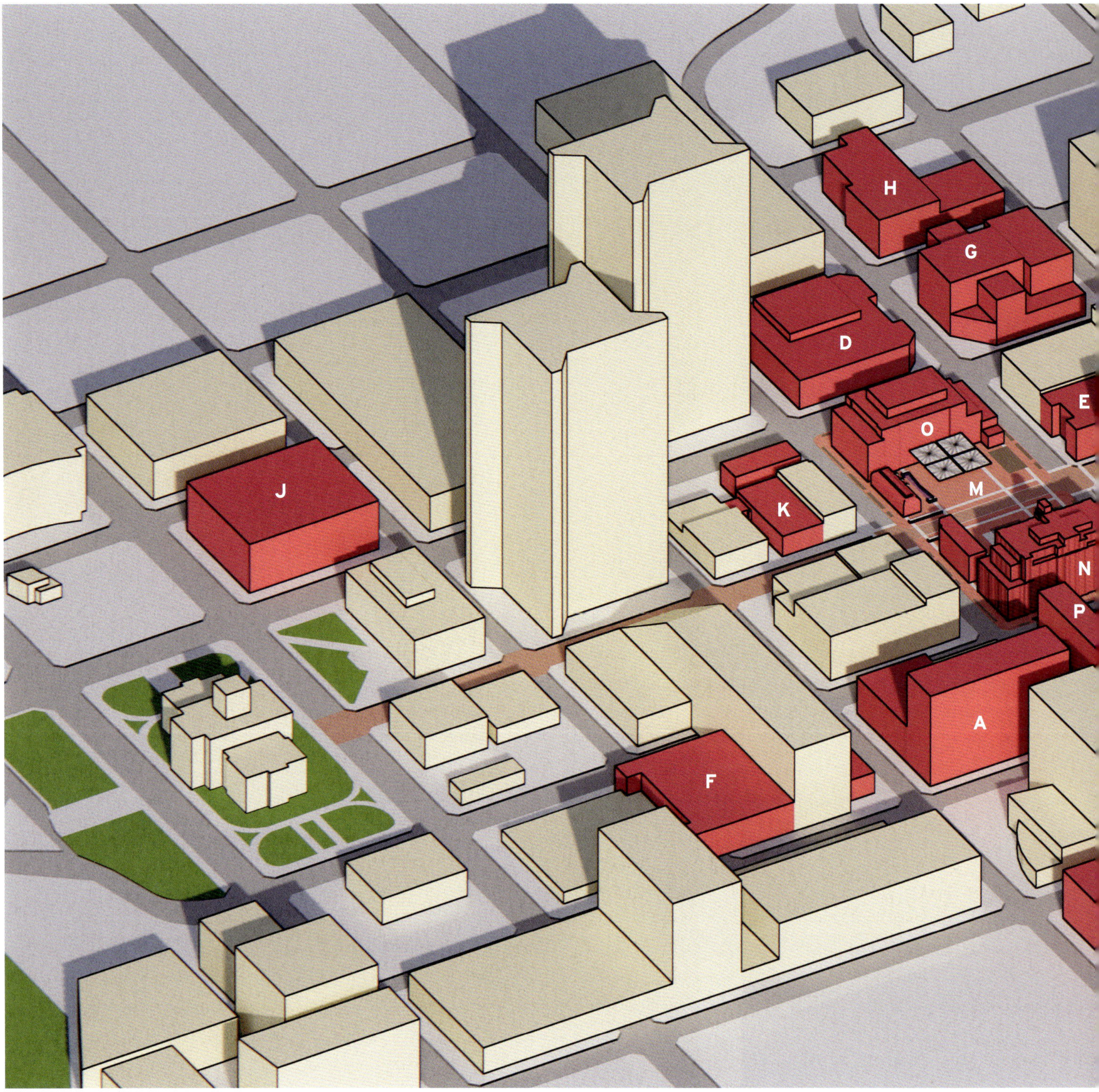

Mixed-use development has continued for decades including the David M. Schwarz–designed Wells Fargo, Sanguinet (now Chase Bank), and Carnegie office buildings, the Sundance Montessori School, and the conversion of the old Sanger department store into loft apartments. The Wells Fargo Building is a four-story infill building. The architects rendered the Sanguinet building in polychromatic brickwork. The Carnegie presents various materials in a subtle palette of grays. And the Montessori school's design precedents are in the Dutch De Stijl movement of the 1910s. Except for the school, all these buildings include ground-floor retail or restaurants, thus increasing visitors to and the vibrancy of the Sundance Square neighborhood. The architects also designed two additional civic structures for Tarrant County Family Law Center and the Lon Evans Corrections Center (see page 186).

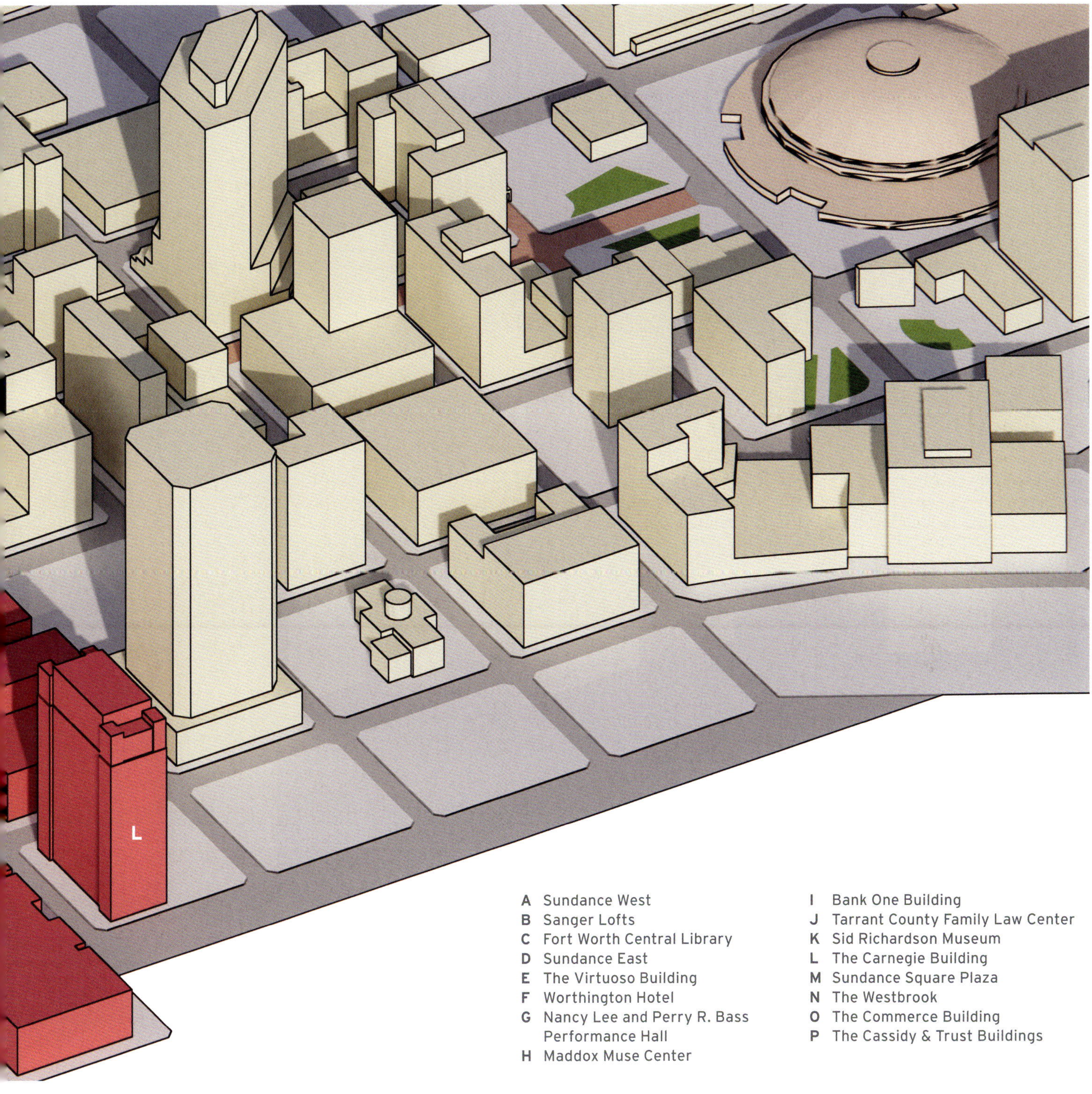

A Sundance West
B Sanger Lofts
C Fort Worth Central Library
D Sundance East
E The Virtuoso Building
F Worthington Hotel
G Nancy Lee and Perry R. Bass Performance Hall
H Maddox Muse Center
I Bank One Building
J Tarrant County Family Law Center
K Sid Richardson Museum
L The Carnegie Building
M Sundance Square Plaza
N The Westbrook
O The Commerce Building
P The Cassidy & Trust Buildings

Lastly, from its earliest days, the Schwarz master plan showed a two-square-block plaza in the middle of the development, spanning Main Street between 3rd and 4th Streets. Concurrent with the eventual execution of this urban park plaza, the Schwarz team added three additional structures. The Westbrook (beige brick; art deco inspired) and Commerce buildings (red brick; traditional) flank the plaza, forming the west and east borders, respectively. Once again, street-level retail and dining are provided in each building. A half block away is the Cassidy, a multiuse building with retail, offices, and a top level of loft apartments. The next chapter has been devoted to the Sundance Square Plaza (see page 130).

Charles Schwab

page 116: The Trust, Cassidy, and the Sanguinet buildings
opposite: Sundance West apartments
this page, top left: Cinema's marquee; **top right and right:** Interior details; **bottom left:** Entrance detail at Sundance West

“There’s a critical marriage between the master plan process and the ownership and operation; the easiest way to say that is that Sundance Square was developed upon urban planning principles mixed with commercial real estate to create a strong and sustainable downtown.”

—Johnny Campbell
President and CEO, Sundance Square

top: Corner of Commerce and 3rd Streets
bottom: AMC palace marquee
opposite: Comedy club façade

KARAOKE
EVERY
FRIDAY
AND
SATURDAY
9PM - 2AM

opposite: Bank One Building
above: Entrance from Throckmorton Street

PARK

opposite: The Carnegie Building
above: Entrance from W 3rd Street

top: The Trust Building
bottom: The Cassidy Building
opposite: Lobby of the Trust Building

SUNDANCE SQUARE PLAZA

Fort Worth, Texas, 2013
Client: Sundance Square Management

From the earliest iteration of the Sundance Square Master Plan in the 1980s, David M. Schwarz Architects always envisioned a two-square-block central plaza in the middle of the neighborhood. The location never varied: the two blocks of surface parking flanking Main Street, bordered by Houston and Commerce Streets, west and east respectively, and 3rd and 4th Streets, north and south respectively. For years, these blocks were cleared of cars and used for the Main Street Festival, outdoor concerts, Christmas celebrations with Santa Claus, boxing matches, movie nights, and other special events. Families just set up their lawn chairs on the hot asphalt. The idea was simple: rather than hard, baking-in-the-Texas-sun macadam, why not develop an urban plaza with appropriate amenities? However, execution proved not as simple. The assumption was that parking was required, and that it would need to be replaced with structured, underground parking beneath the plaza. Furthermore, there was an outparcel in one of the squares. Therefore, realization seemed economically unfeasible. Fast forward a couple decades. The outparcel was acquired, and a study resulted in a decision to disperse parking to the neighborhood's edges. The plaza was finally a viable undertaking.

The architect's design work on Sundance Square Plaza began in earnest. Still, the lots were not blank canvases; there were two small existing buildings, the Jett Building just west of Main on 3rd Street, and the Land Title Building at 4th and Commerce. In order to give the plaza a greater sense of enclosure, the project team added two new offices building to the project: the Westbrook on the western edge (see pages 132 and 133) and the Commerce Building on the eastern edge (see pages 134 and 135). These buildings both have ground-level retail and dining, with most of the restaurants opening onto the plaza and offering outdoor dining. Additionally, the east face of the Westbrook incorporates a fixed stage and an LED clock tower. To balance the mural building—home to the Richard Haas mural honoring Fort Worth as the terminus of the Chisholm Trail—the architects designed a new pavilion across Main Street, which provides a flexible gathering space for various uses and public restrooms for the plaza. The pavilion features massive, horizontally pivoting doors, converting it to an open-air facility in fair weather.

For the plaza itself, the firm teamed with noted landscape architecture firm Michael Vergason Landscape Architects. The plaza design presented two main challenges: accommodating varying numbers of users throughout the day, and ensuring comfort in the searing Texas sun. To address the former, the western half of the plaza incorporates a programmable, basin-less, interactive fountain with 216 jets, set flush with the paving. For the latter, the east half has four very large, mechanized, German umbrellas, each covering 1,250 square feet when deployed. The ground plane is articulated in various paving patterns executed in brick and stone pavers. On rare occasions, like the annual Stock Show Parade, the former Main Street must be opened to vehicular traffic, which was another important design parameter. It had to both look good and function with Main Street either opened or closed. In addition to impacting the separation of the

page 130: Aerial view of the plaza
opposite: Westbrook lobby
top: Westbrook exterior
bottom: View from the plaza

two halves of the plaza, Main Street is delineated with the paving patterns. The design team articulated the plaza's edges with trees, changes in grade, and a wave fountain—which masks traffic noise—so that individuals and small groups can spend time here and feel comfortable in a more intimate setting. All of the aforementioned events are still hosted in the plaza, plus more, with thousands of people in attendance, now enjoying proper accommodations.

above: The Commerce Building at the corner of Commerce and 4th Streets
right: Polychrome brick-decorated lobby of the Commerce Building
opposite: Façade detail incorporating local iconography

this spread: Scenes from Sundance Square Plaza, including the open-air pavilion and the dining porch facing the plaza
following: The square at night with Richard Haas mural

"The plaza created a centerpiece in downtown Fort Worth that had quickly become a destination for North Texas residents and visitors from all around the world. Sundance Square Plaza is a treasure for our city and the response to the pedestrian-friendly plaza has been overwhelmingly positive."

–Johnny Campbell
President and CEO, Sundance Square

SOUTHLAKE TOWN SQUARE

Southlake, Texas, 2013
Client: Sundance Square Management

Prior to David M. Schwarz Architects being commissioned as master planners and design architects for the development, several developers had considered retail projects on the two adjacent farms that eventually became Southlake Town Square. Concerns about receiving the town officials' approval to rezone these properties for commercial development caused many to balk. As the Schwarz team was fresh from a phenomenally successful and public opening of the Ballpark in Arlington, a mere 20 miles to the south, a new developer assumed these architects had the political capital for an effective rezoning effort.

The developer interviewed David Schwarz during a flight from Dallas–Fort Worth to southern California, during which he presented his concept for a "power center" (a collection of "category killer" big-box retailers) along the freeway to the northeast and a neighborhood-serving strip center along the major arterial to the south. Office and civic uses were buried in the center of the site. Mr. Schwarz pointed out that these two uses shared limited overlap in customer base and would result in minimal symbiosis and cross shopping. Furthermore, Southlake had what retailers refer to as near perfect demographics and a severe lack of quality retail establishments. The originally envisioned approach would reduce their potential upside. Moreover, meeting citizens' desires for income-appropriate retail and dining establishments would be key to achieving their support for the project. The Schwarz team was confident they could demonstrate an alternative approach that would have greater long-term value.

The Schwarz team designed the first phase as four blocks of two-story structures—office over retail—on the perimeter of two blocks of publicly accessible parks, one with a bandstand and the other with a fountain. In the first year of operation many national chain stores had their highest-grossing retail sales per square foot at Southlake Town Square, even without the benefit of major department-store anchors. The parks and overall environment were the anchors. The developer convinced the town leaders to move their planned new town hall from a site buried in a one-story shopping center to the Town Square. The architects studied the rich Texas history of grand county courthouses, which were typically in or fronting town squares. This led to their placing the town hall immediately north of the park blocks. Construction commenced on the heels of the first phase's completion. An additional block of office over retail was added, since the town hall would bring more people to the site. For these first two stages of development, the architects employed a variety of architectural expression so that it would not appear to have been designed all at the same time by one designer, unlike typical one-story strip retail. The goal was diversity and a small-town atmosphere with greater human scale and interest, rather than a suburban environment. Moving the majority of the parking to surface lots behind the retail area was a challenging sell to their clients, but a key factor in achieving this goal. They provide a small amount of diagonal "teaser parking," which is why the overall parking scheme works.

For the next phase, the client decided to limit the amount of second-floor office, as they had satisfied most

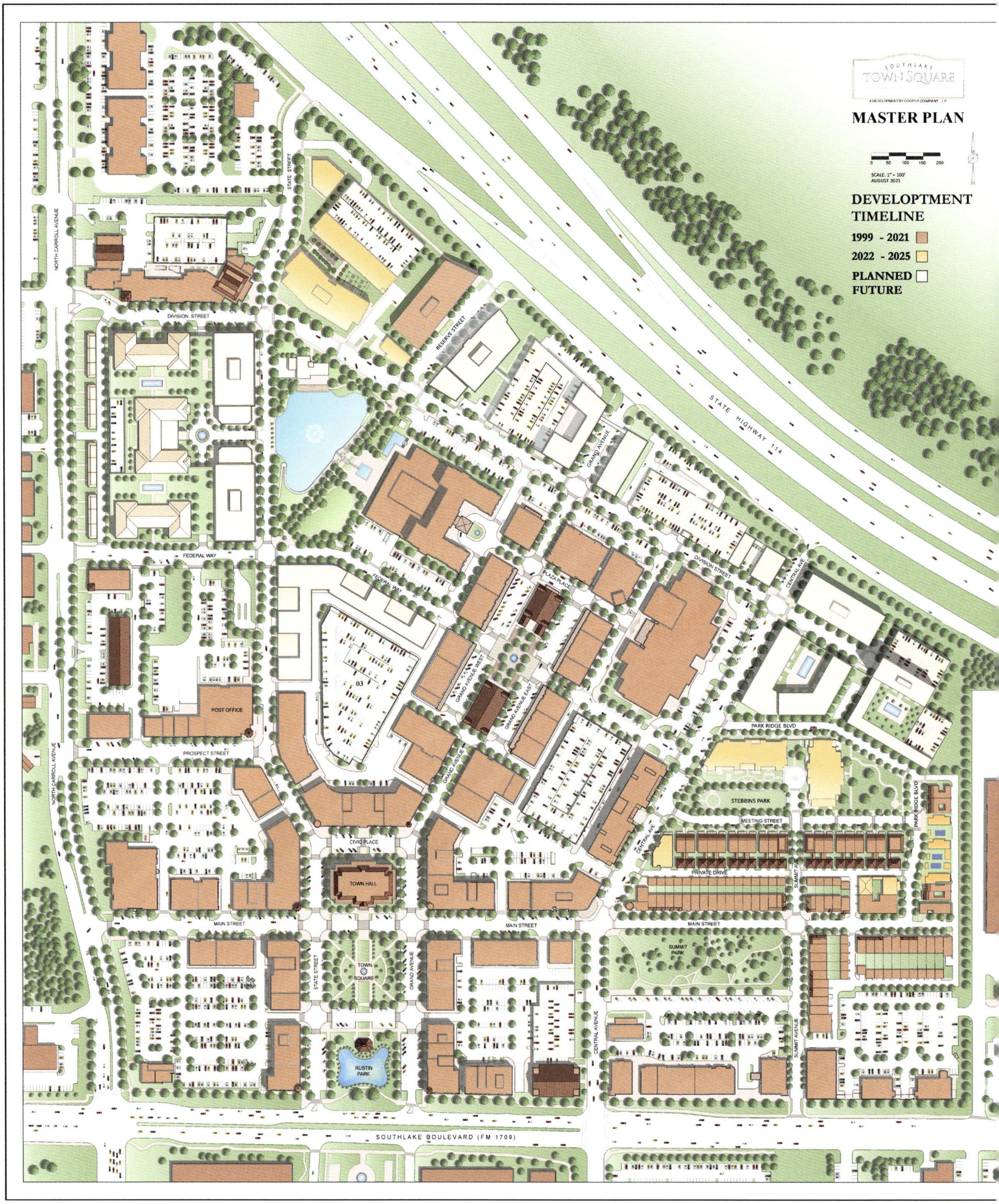
SOUTHLAKE
TOWN SQUARE
A DEVELOPMENT BY COOPER COMPANY L.P.
MASTER PLAN
0 50 100 150 200
SCALE: 1" = 100'
AUGUST 2021
DEVELOPTMENT TIMELINE
1999 - 2021
2022 - 2025
PLANNED FUTURE
STATE HIGHWAY 114
NORTH CARROLL AVENUE
STATE STREET
RESERVE STREET
DIVISION STREET
FEDERAL WAY
GRAND AVENUE
PLAZA PLACE
CENTRAL AVE
POST OFFICE
PROSPECT STREET
PARK RIDGE BLVD
STEBBINS PARK
MEETING STREET
PRIVATE DRIVE
CIVIC PLACE
TOWN HALL
MAIN STREET
SUMMIT PARK
TOWN SQUARE
RUSTIN PARK
CENTRAL AVENUE
SUMMIT AVENUE
SOUTHLAKE BOULEVARD (FM 1709)

page 140: Retail buildings seen from Rustin and Family Park
opposite: Southlake Town Square master plan
this page, top left: Southlake Shake Shack; **top right** Del Frisco's Grille;
bottom Trader Joe's grocery

City of Southlake
GRAND AVE.
City of Southlake
MAIN STREET

City of Southlake
CIVIC PLACE
SMITHBARNEY

SYLVAN LEARNING CENTER
SYLVAN LEARNING CENTER
STATE STREET
BOMBAY

of the demand. A suggestion to add second-floor residential was placed on hold when the city indicated a strong reluctance to approve that. This caused the architects to adjust their design approach. They suggested that this phase be built all at once, and the model for Grand Avenue became colonnaded and arcaded market structures like those found in Havana, Cuba. This phase also included a multiscreen cineplex (designed by others), as an additional anchor, and the development, up to that date, allowed the developers to utilize tax increment financing to build the first structured parking garage for the project. This phase also included a full-service Hilton hotel (designed by others). This addition was testament to the Schwarz team's hypothesis that through careful planning, each phase can enhance the remaining land value and allow for the continuous inclusion of more profitable uses.

Mr. Schwarz always envisioned multifamily residential in close proximity to the retail to make Southlake Town Square a truly walkable, mixed-use community. However, the rest of Southlake is almost exclusively large, single-family homes, so he realized it would be hard to get the needed approvals, and they removed residential from their initial master-plan filing. The project team had to add residential incrementally. The first step was large townhouses, known locally as the Brownstones, fronting two sides of another new park. Shown on the original master plan, this park, on the site's highest ground, was less structured than the previous two, in order to preserve the nicest stand of indigenous trees. As the architects worked in the District of Columbia, with its many historic rowhouse neighborhoods, designing the Brownstones was second nature to them. They employed the same use of detail, rhythms, scaling elements, varieties of brickwork, and varied rooflines as found in this building typology throughout Washington. More recently, purchasers have moved into the Parkview, a condominium building, also designed by the Schwarz team. Additionally, in recent years, the firm has designed several one-off, standalone, purpose-built structures, including a Shake Shack, Del Frisco's Grille, and a Trader Joe's market.

opposite: Retail buildings surrounding Southlake Town Square
above: Pavilion and retail on Grand Avenue
following: The Brownstones and Parkview

CENTRAL AVE

the magnolia

WEST VILLAGE

Dallas, Texas, 2001
Client: Oak Creek Partners, Inc.

Facing a hostile takeover in the mid-1980s, Southland Corporation, the parent company of 7-Eleven convenience stores, completed an ill-fated management buyout. The debt-laden company was severely weakened by the 1987 stock-market crash, and ultimately had to sell its land holdings near North Dallas, on which they had planned Cityplace, a massive 60-acre, mixed-use development. Only one high-rise office building was completed on the east side of the North Central Expressway at the time of the sale. Oak Creek Partners, Ltd. acquired the balance of the land. One of Oak Creek's partners had previously worked with David M. Schwarz Architects, so the newly formed Cityplace Company hired the firm to reimagine Southland's plans for the land west of the expressway. The master plan, which centered around Cityplace Blvd as the main spine, terminated on a site controlled by Henry Miller III. By 1998, a partnership of Henry Miller III (owner of the famed Highland Park Shopping Center in Dallas) and Blake Pogue's Phoenix Property Company formed to develop this 7.6-acre site on the west edge of Cityplace, with the desire to transform the vacant ground into a vibrant, mixed-use neighborhood. They retained the Schwarz firm—this time to design more than 220 apartments above 150,000 square feet of retail space, in the area they dubbed West Village.

First the firm looked at a number of different block and street configurations before settling on the five-block arrangement of the project as built. The pragmatics of screening a large, nearly-800-car garage within the residential component necessitated one larger block, and locating it in the center made it equally accessible to the four perimeter blocks. Budget dictated a fair amount of EIFS (a synthetic stucco) as the exterior finish. Rather than mix it with brick or place EIFS-clad stories above a brick base—pretending that nobody ever looks up—they designed quality brick buildings and made the EIFS façades look like traditional stucco buildings. There were no suburban-looking hybrids. The brick elevations front onto the more prominent, retail-oriented McKinney Avenue and take on a loft-like, converted-commercial appearance. Architects used EIFS on the two interior streets and along the back street, Cole Avenue, which has a predominantly residential character, and where the prevailing material was already stucco.

Economics required that the Landmark movie theaters utilize tilt-wall, concrete construction. The team placed the actual cinemas on the second floor, which freed up the street level for additional retail shops. The architects applied periodic, projecting buildouts along the façade, interspersed with waterjet-cut custom tile inset in vertical recesses, providing articulation and ornamentation on what would have otherwise been a large expanse of blank façade, out of context with the balance of the village.

West Village is also a transit-oriented development. When the Schwarz team started their master planning efforts, the City of Dallas had located three mass transit termini (bus, trolley, and light rail) about 800 feet apart along the North Central Expressway. The architects convinced the City to reconsider its plans and move them all within closer proximity to each other on the same east–west street in the center of Cityplace. This street leads to West Village, thus creating a pedestrian path through the project to the residential neighborhood to the west. The downtown trolley now loops West Village and there are two adjacent light-rail stations.

page 148: Retail corner in West Village
right: Retail buildings of various architectural expressions along tree-lined streets

2000
POLO
RALPH LAUREN

this spread: Residences are located above many of the West Village shops

LOFT
LOFT
LOFT
LOFT

SHARPER

FIREWHEEL TOWN CENTER

Garland, Texas, 2005
Client: Simon Property Group

The Indianapolis-based Simon Property Group, the United States' largest owner of retail properties with over a quarter of a billion square feet of holdings, was keenly aware of the success of David M. Schwarz Architects' Southlake Town Square project (see page 140), so they invited the architects to meet with them. While they were intrigued by its design and early success, Southlake's configuration was anathema to Simon's typical development formula. They asked where the anchors were, and looked highly skeptical when Mr. Schwarz explained that the parks, fountains, benches, and trees were the anchors. The firm didn't hear back ... for a few years, that is. In that period, Simon had been trying to build an enclosed mall in Garland, Texas, northeast of Dallas, but the City of Garland wanted them to build an outdoor "lifestyle center." Simon finally agreed to simply "take the roof off" their current plans, so to speak. They were not as satisfied as they'd hoped to be with their first foray into open-air retail built in the outskirts of Washington, D.C., just up the road from the Schwarz firm's offices. Wanting something different, they returned to the firm for the design of what would be known as Firewheel Town Center.

Simon already had a site plan, and much of it was fixed—especially the position of the anchor department stores. Those plans were still inward focused, owing to the plan's inherent mall DNA. The Schwarz firm endeavored to run one street through and open it up to the perimeter, where they could. Unlike Southlake Town Square, it was mostly one-story retail; although negotiations with the City required the inclusion of 80,000 square feet of second-floor office space. The architects used that space to create additional height on two sides of a small park, which they inserted at the center of the project. For a potential deviation from their Southlake project, the architects initially explored a singular architectural expression, as one can see at the delightful deco/Mission-style Country Club Plaza in Kansas City. After several rounds of study, Simon opted for a more Main Street paradigm of varying building styles, like the approach the architects used at Southlake.

This created a serious challenge: how to create a Southlake-type project on a more limited budget. At Southlake, the budget allowed for three-quarters masonry façades and a quarter EIFS (synthetic stucco) façades. In Garland, the budget required the opposite: 75 percent EIFS and 25 percent brick. Accordingly, the firm had to be extremely judicious in deployment of its limited "brick budget." They did their best to add as much detail to the EIFS as possible, employing premanufactured details that could literally be screwed or glued into place. In a few cases, they even utilized painted details. The firm worked expediently to craft designs for some sixty different façades in the span of barely four months. That actually led to greater stylistic variation than at Southlake. One example (and a firm favorite) is the store initially occupied by Sharper Image (now a Hollister), which combines elements of art moderne with Dutch expressionist architecture. Since the program lacked any type of civic use, the architects spent some of the "brick budget" to create a market building overlooking the park, replete with a clock tower and sloping metal roof. As time

SHARPER IMAGE
SHARPER IMAGE

circuit city
Circuit City
Skin Care & Laser Center

was of the essence, for its front façade, they quoted from themselves, repurposing a façade from their earlier Parker Square project. The project turned out to be better than Simon Property Group had anticipated, and they found they could actually land national retail tenants—who were willing to pay higher rents—with higher brand appeal than they were originally expecting. Once again, the firm showed that good design pays.

page 154: Landscaped spaces between retail buildings
preceding: View along Cedar Sage Drive
this spread: Retail buildings of various architectural expressions along tree-lined streets

Ghirardelli
Ghirardelli
CHOCOLATE
ICE CREAM
CUPC
ICE C
BROOKLY

THE LINQ

Las Vegas, Nevada, 2013
Client: Caesars Entertainment

When private equity firms TPG Capital and Apollo Management acquired controlling interests in what became casino company Caesars Entertainment, David M. Schwarz Architects' long-term client TPG asked them to evaluate existing master plans for the 270 contiguous acres in Las Vegas under Caesars' control. One factor stood out within the architects' lengthy report: the inability to phase the project. The most pressing elements of the plan would need to be built all at once, requiring an investment equal to or greater than what a rival casino company was spending on the City Center project nearing completion. With different investment objectives, the new ownership was not prepared to allocate such resources and asked the Schwarz firm to rethink the master plan.

They immersed themselves in their client's business model and studied the changing trends in casino economics. For the first time ever, patrons were beginning to spend as much money on retail, dining, entertainment, lodging, and other ancillary income streams as they spent on gaming. Two other major factors influenced the replanning. First, too much of Caesars' holdings were of lower-value land to the east along Koval Lane and not directly on The Strip. Second, while Strip visitors loved to walk, despite inhospitable climate most of the year, there were no pleasant pedestrian environments, including along Caesars' Strip frontage. The sidewalks were far too narrow to accommodate all the foot traffic, and obstacles on the sidewalks made them even narrower.

The first project to be executed under the new master plan sought to address these issues. The Linq, as it was called, created a pedestrian-focused retail, dining, and entertainment district, which "linked" The Strip to Caesars' Koval land, thus increasing its value. At first the search for an anchor draw, at the east end of the Linq, focused on a site for a multipurpose arena on Koval. Eventually, that concept was replaced by what in 2014 became the world's tallest observation wheel, the High Roller, standing 550 feet high and located midway between Koval and The Strip. Most of The Strip's development is themed casinos evoking other places: Paris, Rome, New York, Lake Como, Egypt, and other faraway destinations. For the Linq the theme was "Urbanism," and the precedent was not so far away. It was downtown Las Vegas, the pedestrian-oriented, original Las Vegas.

The Linq is a series of interconnected paths and plazas running from The Strip across from the entry to Caesars Palace on the west to the High Roller to the east. A terraced lawn provides access to parking and potential future expansion further east. This promenade replaced a service alley and now restricts vehicular traffic. In plan, the plazas step south to north—that is, the paths enter and exit each plaza at offset locations—yet a line of sight is maintained from beginning to end. To account for a significant change in grade, the plazas are minimally sloped, and while ADA-compliant, the paths make up the remaining grade difference. Paths are delineated with sidewalks and curbs, which provide outdoor dining space, and the plazas run from building face to building face.

Programmatically, the Linq provides additional entrances to three Caesar Entertainment–owned casinos: the Flamingo, the Linq (formerly Imperial Palace and the

SHEAS
CASINO

page 160: The Linq with High Roller Wheel in the distance
opposite: O'Sheas casino entrance
top: Retail along pedestrian walk
bottom: Flamingo casino entrance

Quad) and a relocated O'Sheas. Along its length, there are a wide variety of retail, dining, and entertainment options. To distinguish it from the growth in mall-like indoor shopping centers on The Strip, many of these establishments are new one-off ventures or second locations for successful, innovative startups elsewhere, such as Brooklyn Bowl, Yard House, and Sprinkles Cupcakes. Adjacent to the High Roller is the "Wheel Building," which provides ticketing, queuing, and pre-ride experience for riders of the High Roller, and another adjacent structure houses the Sky Shop, a post-ride gift and logo-wear merchandiser. Architecturally and stylistically, the architects kept the buildings smaller in size to provide a suitable human scale that is ideal for meandering. Most buildings appear to be two stories in height, save for the Wheel Building and Brooklyn Bowl. The firm adopted the storyline—with the client's approval—that the Linq was the remainder of what The Strip's environs may have been before all the casino development if there had been earlier development. As such, they employed a wide array of architectural styles, many traditional, some more modern, and some quite contemporary. These include Victorian and Romanesque masonry structures, classical-revival, simple warehouse-like buildings, art deco, brutalist, art moderne, and an ultra-modern, mullion-less curtain wall addition. Rather than a typical Las Vegas megastructure or ersatz themed attraction, the Schwarz firm want the Linq to appear to have been developed over time and influenced by many hands, much like the pre-Strip Las Vegas downtown.

above and opposite: Retail along the pedestrian walk at dusk

KITSON

AC HOTEL SPARTANBURG
Main St
ONLY

AC HOTEL SPARTANBURG

Spartanburg, South Carolina, 2017
Client: OTO Development

When George Dean Johnson, Jr.'s Johnson Group and OTO Development—its hotel development subsidiary—decided to build a new hotel in downtown Spartanburg, South Carolina, it had to be special. First and foremost, Mr. Johnson was a Spartanburg native, and the headquarters of both companies were less than a half mile away near Morgan Square. Moreover, while OTO had developed hotels under many flags, this would be the first under Marriott's newly acquired AC Hotels brand, founded by Antonio Catalán in Madrid, Spain. Mr. Johnson was both personally and financially invested in further improving downtown Spartanburg, and the AC Hotel Spartanburg would be his next step. He turned to David M. Schwarz Architects for the design. The firm and Mr. Johnson had worked together previously on both the Chapman Cultural Center and the George Dean Johnson, Jr. College of Business and Economics (see pages 312 and 222), as well as a master plan for the Morgan Square area.

The architects looked at several sites at various distances from Morgan Square, some close to the square and others some distance away near the newly emerging entertainment district. The Johnsons chose a site further away from the square to create a terminus to downtown and expand the footprint of what they hoped would become a vibrant pedestrian-oriented area. There was much discussion with the client group about the appropriate height for this building given its location at the far west end of downtown. All agreed that designing a taller, more iconic structure created the visual destination that was needed to better connect this end of Main Street with Morgan Square, Spartanburg's main outdoor gathering place. Thus, they would bracket downtown with two tall structures: the Denny's corporate headquarters to the east and the new hotel to the west. The architects located the building with its through-lobby on the site to respond to two important requirements: first, the need to appropriately address the street and welcome pedestrians in the tradition of grand hotels, and second, to provide a covered vehicular drop-off, on the other side, which was immediately adjacent to the parking lot.

After the firm's standard "taste test" with the clients, the project team selected a traditional, albeit eclectic, design aesthetic, with elements of high-rise reinterpretations of both Georgian Colonial and Italianate precedents. The architects used brick in keeping with Spartanburg's mill-town history and because brick was also used on the firm's earlier projects in Spartanburg. The hotel's tall, one-story base was crafted with cast stone to replicate a traditional limestone edifice. They deployed the same cast stone for additional details up the full height of the structure, including cornices, window heads and sills, balustraded balconettes, quoins, and the rooftop trellises. The front façade is articulated with two towers inset from the quoined corners. The center section has five room bays of double windows, and at the ground floor, a grand metal and glass canopy spans the middle three bays. Above a balustraded entablature, the building's projecting bays are topped with an additional floor with round-headed windows. The architects set back the balance of the top floor and added the flanking trellises in plane with the building face below. The firm crowned this articulate

AC HOTEL

TANBURG
AC

top-floor massing with a multihipped, sloping, orange clay-tile roof, contributing to the building's Italianate read from a distance.

The firm also designed the interior architecture of all the hotel's public spaces, including the entry lobby and reception, bar, and daytime restaurant, which are all interconnected on the ground floor; the suite of meeting rooms situated on the second floor; and the penthouse restaurant and bar perched under the eaves of the rooftop pavilions. These spaces are finished with white marble floors; white-painted, full-height, wood paneling with bolection moldings; and tray ceilings with crown moldings.

page 166: Aerial view from W Main Street
preceding: Entry along W Main Street
above: Detail at parking lot entry
right: Lobby

opposite top: Main lobby
bottom: Interior, rooftop bar
above: Details of rooftop bar

LE GUANAHANI

St. Barthelemy, Ongoing
Client: Le Guanahani

After David Bonderman of the private equity firm Texas Pacific Group (TPG) acquired luxury hotel Le Guanahani from another client of David M. Schwarz Architects, he requested that the firm look at the most effective way to use both the maintenance budget and the capital expenditure budget to improve the property. He had one caveat: the hotel had to remain in operation during peak seasons throughout the renovation. Originally built as a business-class tourist destination, the hotel had fallen behind more luxurious offerings on the island of St-Barth. The property was a collection of common buildings (reception, dining, gym, and the like) and one-, two-, and three-room villas, scattered within the hills and around the beach. The firm's solution was a phased project, over several years, which involved demolishing a couple of rooms, updating and enlarging the remaining guest rooms, and adding a few new rooms, and renovating the common facilities, all to meet current luxury resort expectations.

The architects filled in interstitial spaces and made additions in order to move the bathroom and dressing rooms out of the room proper, and then expanded and refreshed bathrooms. They also added new, larger decks, and worked with designer Luis Pons to develop a new color palette inside and out. This bright scheme of turquoise blue, lavender and bright yellow for the villas and off-white for the public common buildings, was in contrast to other properties on the island, which were moving in a stark, modern, pure white aesthetic. Instead, Le Guanahani reinforced the more indigenous Caribbean Creole vernacular. The buildings had simple wood cladding and trim, with exposed ceilings of heavy rafters and perpendicular planks. The design team added traditional, hinged, solid-wood window shutters to the renovated and new structures and replaced many of the floors with Ipe planks. The walls were painted plaster over solid concrete, and all have painted wood cornices to define the room and provide a location to conceal LED lighting and curtain tracks. New bathrooms have honey-colored, mosaic tiles and freestanding, dark wood and cane vanities. Mr. Pons also developed a storyline for the property based on international travelers, and he designed a suite of furniture to reinforce this theme. The renovations also involved significant site work and landscaping. Most patrons had traveled between buildings on the road system, which was less than a pleasant experience. To correct this, the firm revamped the systems of pathways and added lush native plantings to enhance the pedestrian experience throughout the resort. To augment the existing beach on the Grand Cul-de-Sac Cove and expand the resort's beach frontage, the owners acquired an adjacent piece of property, and the design team developed a new beach, Marigot, on Maréchal Cove.

In September 2017, as the Schwarz team was designing the last major phase of renovation involving changes to the hotel's food service, Hurricane Irma devastated St-Barth with a direct hit. Irma destroyed one-third of Le Guanahani, considerably damaged another third, and barely touched the remainder, save for vegetation, which the storm severely damaged throughout. The third nearest the beach was hardest hit. While nobody should call a natural disaster of this magnitude fortunate in any sense

of that word, it did provide an opportunity to correct inherent problems with the beach's existing layout and structures. The restaurant—in the wrong location on the beach—and kitchen were much too small most of the time and too large at lunch. The beach was too small, and the beach villas lacked privacy. The architects relocated the gym, and converted that structure to a new two-bedroom suite. They replaced the restaurant with a new structure in a different location in order to expand the beach, and they moved the beach villas up the hill to improve the views, increase privacy via vertical separation, and reduce the possibility of future flooding. The new Beach House restaurant features indoor and outdoor dining, with two separate indoor dining rooms to maintain an intimate scale and provide different dining experiences. The architects added a dedicated lounge to the restaurant program and located the boutique in an adjacent central position. Both dining rooms have an indoor/outdoor feel with large sliding glass panels that can be closed in inclement weather. The materials build upon the property standards with Ipe wood floors, interior wood siding, and fabric-wrapped wall panels. One of the dining rooms has an open grill kitchen with a wood-burning pizza oven. They also reprised the popular "feet in the sand" lunch restaurant with the its iconic white fabric sails. Lastly, the team replaced and upgraded outdated infrastructure, which suffered from long-deferred maintenance, and planned a robust replanting replacement program throughout the property.

page 174: Beach House dining room
above: Beach House bar

clockwise from top left: Beach House pool deck; Lagoon Suite; Typical guest room
following: Aerial view

CIVIC, HEALTHCARE, & EDUCATION

CITY OF SOUTHLAKE &
1400 MAIN S

SOUTHLAKE TOWN HALL

Southlake, Texas, 1999
Client: City of Southlake

While David M. Schwarz Architects were well into their master planning efforts for Southlake Town Square (see page 140), the city of Southlake was planning a new campus-style, one-story, town hall on the back side of a strip mall at a remotely located suburban development. Meanwhile, the Schwarz firm's client, Cooper and Stebbins, was looking for another draw for the town square development. The architects produced a quick rendering to help their client market the idea to the mayor and council. The mayor quickly became a big proponent of the project.

At that point, the plans showed three open blocks in the center of the first phase. The one closest to Southlake Boulevard, the town's main artery, was reserved for future commercial development and the other two blocks to the north would become dedicated parks. However, the city wanted the northernmost block for the town hall and wanted the two park blocks to remain open to Southlake Boulevard. The architects modified the plan, and Cooper and Stebbins then sold the municipality the block for the grand sum of one dollar.

The architects had one significant concern: with 80,000 square feet of programmed space—requiring four stories and 200 feet in length—they had to ensure the building would overwhelm neither the parks nor the surrounding two-story commercial buildings. The architects employed many design devices to mitigate the building's mass. First, a rise in grade, south to north, allowed them to depress the structure by two-thirds of a floor, yet daylight the lowest level on the north side. That also provided barrier-free access from the north despite the elevated portico on the south. Next, they divided the park-facing façade into five parts: a center mass, two hyphens, and two end bays. They further divided the central portion into five parts: a three-bay portico, flanked by hyphens with double windows, and ending with projecting outboard bays. The central portion reads as three stories with an English basement, except at the outer bays, which are without the top floor. On the hyphens, they set back the top floor to create a two-story with attic read, and at the outermost bays they eliminate the fourth floor altogether.

After studying courthouses and city halls, near and far, in the state of Texas (a proud architectural history, indeed), the architects arrived at a Romanesque-influenced, brick and stone vernacular for the building's exterior appearance. This resonated well with the mayor and council. Design components included the aforementioned portico, a corbelled brick cornice, arch-headed windows at the third floor, projecting balconettes, and cast spandrel panels. As a nod to this structure's civic purpose, the Texas lone star adorns both the spandrel panels and the portico's entablature. Taking a move straight out of the movie *Back to the Future,* the architects added a clock face in the brick pediment above the portico.

Internally, they arranged the program around a two-story, colonnaded atrium. With entries at both ends, in addition to servings as the main circulation spine of the building, the atrium also acts as an indoor extension of the park blocks. The city uses this "indoor town square" as a space for receptions, early voting, and other civic events. On the main level, east of the atrium is the council chambers; to the west is a municipal courtroom.

The atrium is finished with pattern terrazzo flooring, mahogany doors, painted wood wainscotting with panels above, more lone stars on the entablature, and coffered ceilings. Many of these details continue in the courtroom and chambers, where the architects used more clear-finished woodwork for the judge's and council's daises, respectively. Southlake's first public library occupies part of the lower level, occupying expansion space for the city, until the library outgrows this space and moves into its own building.

page 182: Façade detail
above: View from across Stebbins Park
right: City council chamber
opposite: View through lobby to park beyond

COUNCIL CHAMBERS
COUNCIL CHAMBERS

TARRANT COUNTY COURTS AND CRIMINAL JUSTICE FACILITIES

Fort Worth, Texas, 2005
Client: Tarrant County, Texas

Concurrent with David M. Schwarz Architects' other work in downtown Fort Worth's Sundance Square neighborhood (see page 116), Tarrant County hired the architects to design two civic structures in that area. The first was the Tarrant County Family Law Center; the second was the Lon Evans Corrections Center. The architects developed a very interesting, temple-in-the-sky plan (where the mid-section shaft of the building is capped with a temple-like form) for the Family Law Center, which was originally going to house both civil and family courts. However, the county removed the civil court functions after another project—designed by others but funded by the same bond referendum—came in over budget. The firm had to rethink the concept, as it was less suited for a shorter building. The architects turned to the historic Tarrant County Courthouse of 1895 for inspiration. However, rather than producing an all-granite building like the Texas Sunset Pink courthouse, the architects mixed this granite with rich red brickwork. For economy, they varied the ratio of granite versus brick on the various façades. The main west façade, facing the original courthouse and Sundance Square, had the most granite. The architects reduced the amount of granite on the east and west façades and used limited amounts on the less important south façade. Although lacking the arch-headed windows and obvious Richardsonian Romanesque character of the historic courthouse, the Family Law Center's details pay homage to its predecessor. However, here the details—such as the brackets, stone mullions, cornices, triglyphs, spandrel panels, and granite inserts—are actually a modern reinterpretation of the more traditional antecedents. For instance, the spandrel panels have limited depth changes, but incorporate several different granite textures for additional interest. They also have sandblasted Scales of Justice to telegraph the building's mission. Overall, this use of ornament and detail gives the building a transitional appearance between traditional and modern.

The emotional nature of the proceedings in a family court, unlike a criminal court, can at times result in it becoming the scene of a felony, and hence the need for heightened security. Inside the recessed north entry vestibule, a secure lobby leads to a monumental stairway up to a central atrium. The balance of the ground floor, accessed by a separate entry, is dedicated to the IV-D courtrooms and support spaces; IV-D refers to the Texas Criminal Code section dealing with unpaid child support payments. On the top four floors, the architects arranged the remaining program around two two-story atria, stacked on top of each other. The upper one is skylighted. Miscellaneous court offices, such as Family Services and the District Attorney's Protective Unit, are on the second floor; the clerk's office is on the third. Courtrooms ring the atrium on floors four and five. The atria feature patterned terrazzo flooring, green granite wainscotting with fabric paneled walls above, decorative metal railings, and coffered ceilings. There are two types of courtrooms: district courtrooms for elected district court judges, and associate courtrooms. The district court proceedings often last longer and occasionally hold jury trials. Therefore, the Schwarz team advocated strongly for windows in all the district courtrooms. As the jury trials

TARRANT COUNTY FAMILY LAW CENTER

are somewhat rare, the architects placed the often-empty jury boxes in alcoves on the sides of these courtrooms. They designed many of the central elements of these courtrooms—judge's dais, witness stands, and jury box parterre wall—out of clear-finished species of mahogany, which add an appropriate level of grandeur to this very important civic function.

For the Lon Evans Corrections Center, the county returned to David M. Schwarz Architects at the urging of the Fort Worth city officials. As the Family Law Center, at completion, had cost $5 million dollars less than the contractor's guaranteed maximum price and the county's project personnel were happy with the firm's services, they readily agreed. In fact, the Lon Evans building was to be an annex to the county's less-than-friendly high-rise urban correctional facility (UFCs as they were known), completed barely two decades earlier. The city urged the county to make the annex more humanist and pedestrian-friendly. As the interiors comprise prefabricated, welded, stainless-steel cells, the firm's involvement in their design was very limited, save for getting the specialty prison architects to abandon an earlier arrangement, which would have required a ziggurat-like massing. It was important to the Schwarz team that the massing was in keeping with the country's history of architecturally great urban prisons that they studied at the beginning of the commission. They felt that jails should reflect the gravity of their public purpose. To relay that purpose to the public, who hope they never need to enter the jail, the architects include a cast-stone frieze at the top of the street façades, which incorporates a repetition of steer heads juxtaposed with a stylized lock and key motif. While using a different, more economical brick, the new corrections center reflects both the landmark courthouse and the Family Law Center with its use of the Texas Sunset Pink granite. Inset, framed panels in the granite base continue the incarceration iconography with more locks and keys, along with the local iconography of lone stars and steer heads—the county's and city's symbols, respectively.

page 186: Court building with historic courthouse beyond
opposite: Main entry
above: Typical courtroom view

left: Correctional center
above (top): Façade details; **(bottom):** Bas-relief panel

ALPHARETT

ALPHARETTA CITY HALL

Alpharetta, Georgia, 2014
Client: City of Alpharetta, Georgia

The Alpharetta City Hall project started with an open request for proposals issued by the City of Alpharetta in Georgia for both the design of the city hall and surrounding master plan for a city-controlled parcel of land to be known as City Center. The old historic downtown—or more precisely, what remained of it—was on the opposite (west) side of Route 9, also known as South Main Street. After David M. Schwarz Architects submitted their proposal, the city invited them for an interview.

The interview turned out to be a case study for speaking one's mind and saying what one thinks. The city had done some pre-planning showing the city hall and future development in a park-like setting. The firm knew that while this might be acceptable for the city hall, the commercial development, especially the retail, would not work without street frontage. So, for the interview, they showed an alternate arrangement, along with examples of the firm's work that were similar and had indeed proved successful. For the interview, they showed a street perpendicular to South Main Street, which provided for future four-story private development, with adequate visibility and access. The Schwarz team catapulted from fourth place, before the interview, into first place, and the city hired them for the commission. During the master planning phase, to link the new development to the old downtown, the architects provided a new village green, which is open to South Main Street. At the east end of the green, a cross street linked a pair of one-way streets on north and south sides into a single, two-way street that centered on the site for the city hall. These streets formed a small grid for the four blocks of private development east of the green and west of City Hall.

The architects placed City Hall itself at the east end and low point of a sloping site, with City Center to the west and a new public park to the east. The building makes up the grade change with the main floor at grade facing Main Street and the lower level opening to the new park. As they often do, the architects presented the core client group—the mayor and a few council members—with what they refer to as a taste test. They compiled photos of various city halls, courthouses, and other public buildings all throughout the state of Georgia and reviewed them with the clients. These civic leaders, especially the mayor, expressed a strong predilection for the most traditional precedents. Thus, the architects based their design on a Georgian vocabulary of details and materials. Interestingly, Alpharetta City Hall is the second project on which the architects turned to the movie *Back to the Future* for inspiration, the first being Southlake Town Square. In the movie, the director used "Courthouse Square," a set on the back lot of Universal Studios in California. Having appeared in over fifty movies from 1948 through 2021, it can lay claim to being America's paradigmatic courthouse. Alpharetta City Hall, designed with red brick and beige stone, has traditional elements like arched windows, stone quoins, turned balustrades, classical entablatures, and stone window surrounds. A three bay, two-story portico sits in front of a three-story central mass topped with a pediment. Behind this mass sits a domed cupola. To each side of the center sits additional three-story masses (albeit absent pediments), which the

Alpharetta
Celebrates
Arbor Day!

architects set back a couple of feet from the central mass. Outboard of these are two-story wings.

Internally, on the more public main and second levels, the architects arranged the program around a two-story oval atrium. Front and back halls connect entry vestibules to the atrium, effectively forming a through lobby with the back door accessing a raised porch overlooking the park. The designers arranged the council chambers, a pre-function space, and a multipurpose room on a cross-axis to the atrium space. They used compatible traditional detail for these public spaces, designing walnut paneled wainscotting and trim. Additional city administration spaces are around the atrium on the second floor. The mayor's suite and more administrative offices are on the smaller third floor and the attic behind the pediment houses mechanical equipment. This stepping of the floor sizes, wedding caking so to speak, gives the building overall greater height and increases its visibility from South Main and the village green.

page 192: Column detail
preceding: Front façade
opposite: Rotunda
above: City Council chamber

Cook Children's
Dodson Specialty Clinics
1500 Cooper Street
EMERGENCY
Emergencia
Medical Center Main Entrance
Dodson Specialty Clinics

COOK CHILDREN'S MEDICAL CENTER

Fort Worth, Texas, Ongoing
Client: Cook Children's Medical Center

The Cook Children's Health Care System in Texas has been David M. Schwarz Architects' longest, nearly continuous, institutional client. Since beginning design work on the original, new 183-bed, seven-story hospital, the firm has not gone more than a year and a half without working on either a new building, addition, or master-plan update. As of this book's publication, they were working on three projects either in design or construction.

It all started in 1985 with a simple idea after the 1983 merger of Fort Worth's two children's hospitals. Founding chairman, Robert M. Bass, held the premise that given equal quality of medical care, parents would take their sick or injured child to the facility that offered the more pleasant and comforting environment. That became the guiding principle for over thirty-five years of health-care design. Cook and the architects took the approach that the needs of patients and their families were as important in caregiving as was satisfying the requirements of doctors and medical staff. How could the hospital be child-friendly, and in places childlike, without being childish? How to give equal weight to science, medicine, comfort, and quietude? The answers involved natural light everywhere including the cafeteria, pictographs incorporated into signage, a soft palette of colors and materials, and no dead-end public corridors. To accomplish this last need, the architects had to demonstrate that there would be no loss of efficiency, which in hospitals is measured in nursing steps per hour. Their plan actually reduced these steps by five compared to an earlier plan by others. Furthermore, scary-looking equipment, such as monitors and head-wall gas terminals, could be hidden when not in use. Lastly, the architects provided a variety of public and private spaces, where families could seek solidarity or solitude, respectively, as they desired.

Mr. Bass also wanted to ensure the quality of ongoing development, well into the foreseeable future. He realized the value of a good master plan, as did subsequent board and administrative leadership. Cook is perhaps the most coherent medical campus in the country, thanks in large part to that master plan, which is part of the hospital's endowment. After each construction project, the hospital has retained the Schwarz firm to update the master plan in concert with their efforts to anticipate future needs in the everchanging health-care environment and business climate. With every revision, the architects considered not only the next and future building, but also what they refer to as the negative space, the gardens, the open spaces between the buildings, and pedestrian and vehicular circulation. Through the decades, they also utilized a consistent palette of exterior materials and details, rather than making each phase a new architectural statement. These included items now part of the Cook signature brand: blue pyramidal roofs and window mullions, Texas beige limestone, two colors of glazed masonry units, and metal canopies and porte cocheres supported by tapered pylons. Although they returned to these design motifs and color schemes, the architects evolved the materiality and construction techniques in step with advancing building technologies and new economically beneficial materials and systems. Growth of the main Fort Worth campus includes medical office buildings, several parking garages,

page 198: Central bay of the main hospital building
preceding: View across central court showing additions
above: Dodson Specialty Clinics

central mechanical plants, outpatient clinics, expansion of the two-story base, and two new patient towers.

The team continued the homogeneity and familiarity on the interior. The original hospital was arranged around a skylighted central atrium, where patients—those well enough to do so, but too sick to go home—could celebrate the holidays with family. Moreover, a transverse "Main Street" links entries and lobbies throughout the complex with each other and with ground-level areas for specialty services. The medical center's lobbies and Main Street are designed with timeless and durable finishes, like stone and terrazzo floors, loads of natural light, and a mixture of stylized, classically inspired architectural details created with a bit of whimsy to delight both children and adults. Since then, every attached expansion has included some form of central space, all linked by a pedestrian-friendly extension of Main Street. Both patrons and staff can utilize Main Street, other public corridors, and bridges to get from one part of the campus to any other part without going outdoors, yet the landscape equally accommodates those that wish to spend some time outdoors.

above: Playground
opposite (top): Main hospital atrium;
(bottom): Typical interior views

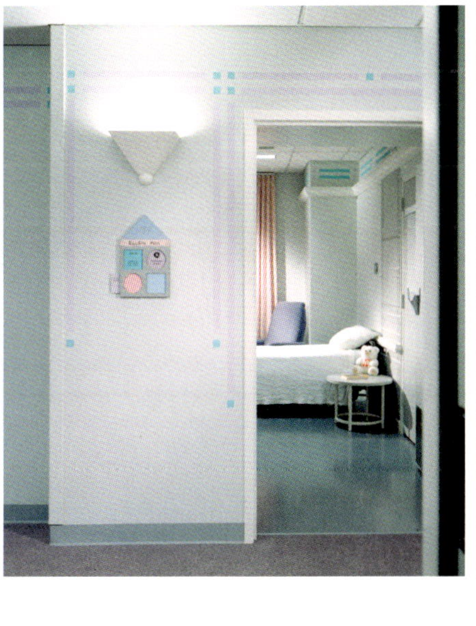

this spread: Views along the extension of the hospital's "Main Street"

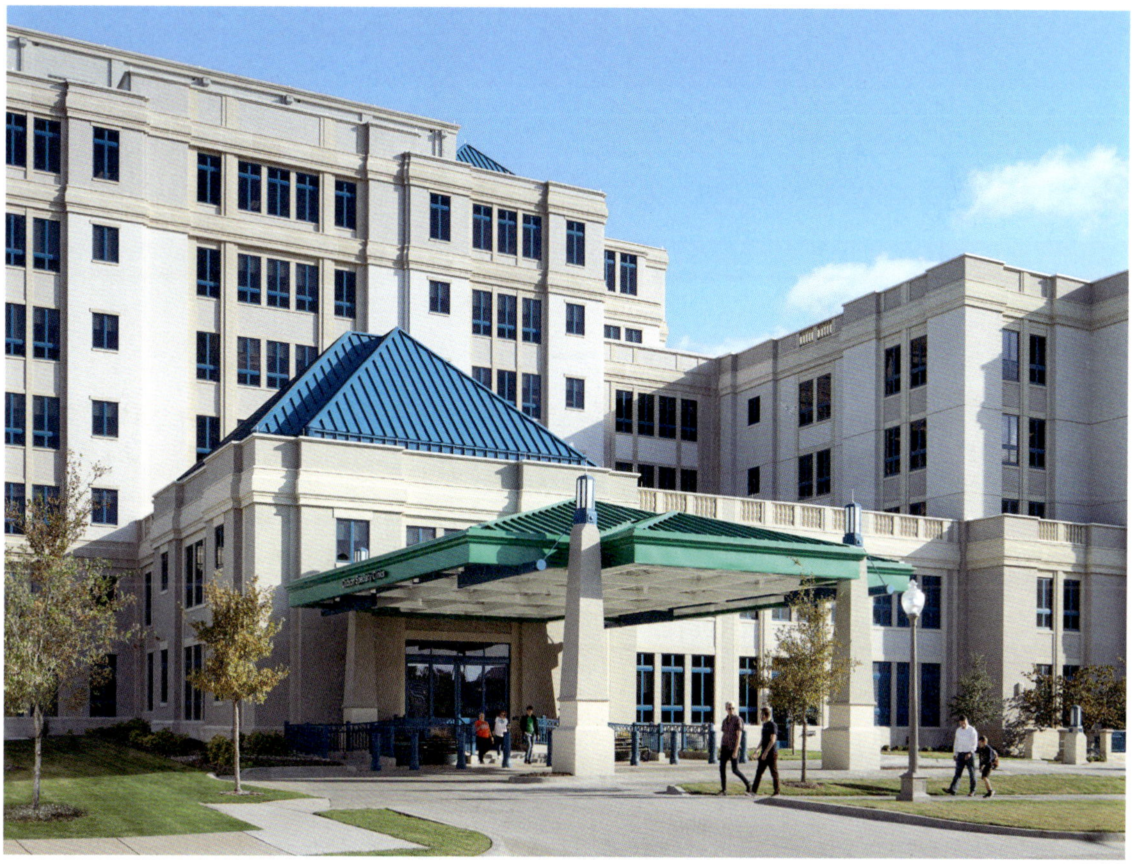

opposite: Dodson expansion, atrium
top: Dodson expansion, west façade
bottom: Dodson expansion, entry on south façade

YALE CLASS OF '54 ENVIRONMENTAL SCIENCE CENTER

New Haven, Connecticut, 2001
Client: Yale University

The sciences have been somewhat of an afterthought at Yale College over the years. The early-twentieth-century buildings—marking the area currently referred to as Science Hill—included buildings for the chemistry and biology departments, along with the Peabody Museum of Natural History, which were all oriented to the street. In the 1950s and '60s, numerous new buildings were added to the center of the block, with little or no concern about the spaces between them. This is antithetical to the balance of Yale's campus, and served to further reinforce the notion of Science Hill as a satellite of the Yale campus with its beautiful courtyards and quads just a third of a mile to the south. When Yale retained David M. Schwarz Architects to design a building for a new interdisciplinary program for the environmental sciences, its site at the foot of Science Hill on Sachem Street simultaneously presented both an opportunity and a challenge. How could the building, which would replace an inappropriate 1950s addition to the Peabody, help reconnect Science Hill to the Yale campus?

The Class of '54 Environmental Science Center, as it was named, sits between the Peabody and Sachem Wood. As the Yale Colleges are traditional collegiate Gothic in style and most of Science Hill is modern, the architects sought a transitional expression to relate to both aesthetics. While using the collegiate Gothic as precedent, they avoided merely copying that style. They combined a massing that was inherently Gothic with an execution and details that were subtly more complex and modern. At first glance it appears Gothic, but upon further study it is of its own time. The firm placed a tower—an element common to many of the Yale campus buildings—at the corner of Sachem Street and the bottom of the Wood. The building's exterior is highly stylized, predominately brick, and reinterprets its precedents in a more monochromatic and tauter manner. In addition to the tower, design components include bays with gable tops, pilasters topped with finials, an oriel, and slate mansard roofs. Functionally, the tower top and mansards mask views of the laboratory's mechanical ventilation from the high point of Sachem Wood. The field brick is rich red, laid in Flemish bond with contrasting, salt-glazed, ironspot brick headers. The degree of contrast, and thus overall appearance, changes over the course of a day due to varying sun angles. The architects used red cast stone to replicate sandstone for the base, window surrounds, belt courses, spandrel panels, and tower accents, much of it set flush with the brickwork, in contrast to historic Gothic structures.

The Environmental Science Center houses laboratories for departments focused on a range of environmental research, including ecology and evolutionary biology, geology and geophysics, anthropology, and environmental studies. As per the program, the architects connected the new building to the Peabody, where it provides collection storage, collection management, and research space for scholars using the Peabody's collection of specimens. Additionally, the building includes faculty offices and teaching spaces. The firm arranged the interior along a three-story, skylit shaft—quite modern in feel and appearance—that separates the labs from the collections' spaces. Fritted glass allows highly controlled and filtered

natural light into the work rooms, but not into the light-sensitive storage space for the collections. On the lab side of the corridor, where it connects the interior spaces, there is a glazed, tile wainscot to protect the walls from the carts that frequently travel along the corridor. Such tile work is also a hallmark of many of the university's historic interiors. In the ground-floor public areas, the architects designed the wainscot panels using Texas Shell Stone, a limestone, which contains prehistoric fossils from when the shores of the Gulf of Mexico reached what is now the Hill Country outside of Austin, Texas. In a break from convention, the Schwarz firm advocated turning the typical rectangular lab module on its side, so that natural light would benefit graduate students spending long hours there. Although it was completed before the widespread adoption of Leaders in Energy and Environment Design standards, at completion the building proved to be one of the most energy-efficient lab facilities—a building type that is generally not very efficient—on the Yale campus.

page 210: Tower at entry
preceding: Sciences center with historic context beyond
opposite: Typical interior views, including vertical circulation, corridors, and atrium
above: Naturally lit lab spaces

Holtrey Pool
13FT-6IN
13FT-6IN

HAWKEN SCHOOL NATATORIUM

Gates Mills, Ohio, 2003
Client: The Hawken School

In 1999, as construction on the Cleveland Orchestra's Severance Hall was nearing completion, there was significant overlap between the boards of Hawken School, an independent school, and the orchestra. In fact, a member of the school's board and a member of the orchestra's renovation committee were married to each other. So, when the school wanted to build a new facility for their renowned swim team, the Hawken School Natatorium, they naturally turned to David M. Schwarz Architects. Hawken School was divided into the lower and middle school in Lyndhurst, Ohio, and the upper school campus in Gates Mills, Ohio. Each campus had one landmark structure—Bolton Hall in Lyndhurst and the White House (home of Thomas White, founder of White Motor Company). Unfortunately, on each campus these landmarks were surrounded by less-than-ideal newer school structures. This was particularly problematic at the upper school, where the athletic facilities created an unwelcoming and inappropriate first impression of the campus. The board chair described it as an overscale porch without a front door. Concurrent with commencement of design work on the pool project, the firm was also retained to master plan both campuses, with a goal of correcting past errors. The school adopted the architects' suggestion that its milieu should teach visual literacy and prepare its students to be educated stewards of the built environment. The pool project was the first project completed under these master plans.

The Hawken swim teams were perennial state champions, and included Olympians and world record holders. This success came despite training on the lower-school campus in a former outdoor pool that was later enclosed with an A-frame structure. School leadership determined that the new facility at Gates Mills was a priority. As swimming was part of the overall athletic program, locating the pool adjacent to the athletic complex created an opportunity to fix the campus's arrival experience. With very little selective demolition of the existing structures, the Schwarz firm was able to use the new pool facility to mask the "doorless porch." Gates Mills is in a part of eastern Ohio known as the Western Reserve as it was originally the western reserve of Connecticut. As such, a unique architectural style of Colonial architectural, known as Western Reserve, which is more similar to New England than Midwestern design, is prevalent throughout the community. In fact, the White House and the few remaining original structures from the White estate are examples of the Western Reserve style, exhibiting wood framing; white clapboard and/or shingles; dark gray, steep-sloped roofs; and simple, elegant, Greek Revival detailing. The architects employed this palette on the new building, forming an important link to the estate's finer architectural past.

The pool itself has all of the state-of-the-art features necessary to keep the swim team competitive at the highest level, such as the ideal depth; high-tech, no-splash-back gutters; and sophisticated temperature and humidity control. A grandstand provides seating for teammates, family, and friends. However, while the swim team is celebrated throughout the school, a very small percentage of students actually participate on the team. Therefore, it was important that the facility also address the needs

of the greater student body. Behind a new, appropriately scaled front porch on the stepping triple-gabled entry façade, the architects placed a new common lobby. This lobby links the swimming pool, the old gymnasium, and what was known as the new gym, thus serving a much larger population of student athletes. The new porch and lobby also serve as a secondary student commons and convenient waiting spaces for those being picked up by parents at the conclusion of after-school activities. Lastly, a new corridor with large windows into the pool enclosure links the shared lobby to the other side of the complex where a reopened entry faces the White House.

page 216: Natatorium interior
preceding: Natatorium exterior
opposite: Detail of gable and cupola
above and left: Common spaces

GEORGE DEAN JOHNSON, JR. COLLEGE OF BUSINESS AND ECONOMICS

Spartanburg, South Carolina, 2010
Client: University of South Carolina Upstate

When the University of South Carolina Upstate approached George Johnson, a successful investor and Spartanburg, South Carolina native, about a significant contribution toward building an undergraduate business school on its suburban Spartanburg campus, he readily agreed with one major caveat: the building had to be located in downtown Spartanburg. Mr. Johnson's businesses were headquartered in Spartanburg's downtown, and he was on a mission to revitalize it. Eager to advance its program, the university agreed. As David M. Schwarz Architects had designed the recently completed and highly successful Chapman Cultural Center (see page 312), Mr. Johnson persuaded the school to hire the firm as design architects. The architects had also worked with Mr. Johnson on a master plan for parts of downtown, which among other features, showed St. John Street as a pedestrian-friendly link between Barnet Park and the center of downtown. With Mr. Johnson's assistance, the school procured a site on St. John Street, adjacent to the Chapman Cultural Center.

The architects decided to employ a hybrid of architectural expressions. As collegiate Gothic has been associated with quality education for almost a millennium, for the main entry—at the southeast corner of North Liberty Street, across from the cultural center—the firm designed a stylized, collegiate Gothic tower, which is suggestive of their design of Yale University's Class of '54 Environmental Science Center (see page 210). The Flemish bond brickwork with glazed headers, the dark red cast-stone details, the bays with chamfered corners, and the polychromatic brick accents are all reminiscent of their Gothic precedents, but the overall expression of the balance of the exterior has a compatible, yet distinctly different, read than the tower. The fenestration is more modern, with large two-story windows and green metal spandrel panels, recalling those of the Chapman's brick buildings to the east. As a precedent, those buildings employed the Auditors Building of the Bureau of Engraving and Printing complex (adjacent to the United State Holocaust Memorial Museum) in Washington, which has a blend of Victorian-Gothic and Romanesque-Revival elements. The team elected to keep the building's base and adjacent sidewalk level with its corners in hope that the city will eventually remove a dip in the roadway, a remnant of an abandoned railway overpass. The same façade design and materials turn the corner and extend along North Liberty Street. Although the rear façade, which faces a new parking garage, has similar fenestration, the architects switched to a stucco system for economy. Nevertheless, the space between the garage and the business school is well landscaped and serves as an outdoor gathering spot for students.

The architects arranged and detailed the interiors to maximize natural light. Windows, skylighted lobbies and lounges, and glazed breakout rooms and galleries, provide borrowed natural light to almost every space. In addition, the galleries are not merely galleries in name only: Mr. Johnson has lent part of his noteworthy Art of the American South collection to enliven these multipurpose spaces. The architects also helped the school develop educational program features such as a dedicated mock stock-trading room with state-of-the-art technology;

page 222: Common spaces linking classrooms and offices
left: Façade along East St. John's Street with Chapman Cultural Center at right
above: Polychrome and red sandstone detail

opposite: Octagonal atrium
left: Vertical circulation
bottom: Sequence of common spaces

a large, tiered assembly hall underwritten with funds from BMW; flexible classrooms that can be configured to work with various teaching styles; and faculty offices adjacent to classrooms to encourage student–faculty interaction. The building also includes free "incubator" office space for recent graduates to encourage start-up businesses. The firm selected interior materials for their economy and serviceability; however, the architects still endeavored to provide faculty and students with a delightful environment. Stairways are open and filled with light. Railings and parapets are metal and glass with natural wood for the handrails. Light fixtures and furniture are playful. The highly durable terrazzo floors have intricate patterns with borders incorporating symbols of world currencies as polished metal inserts. The George, as they call it for short, has become a model for undergraduate business-school buildings, with others contemplating new facilities visiting on a regular basis.

E. Bronson Ingram College
It would be a mistake if
we contented ourselves
with a backward look.
In building a university
there is never an occasion
for finishing touches.
The task is always one of
laying foundations.
James H. Kirkland
Chancellor, 1893-1937

VANDERBILT UNIVERSITY RESIDENTIAL COLLEGES

Nashville, Tennessee, Ongoing
Client: Vanderbilt University

David M. Schwarz Architects first started working with Vanderbilt University in 2003, when then board chairperson, Martha Ingram—also chair of the Nashville Symphony Orchestra's board, for whom the firm was designing a new concert hall (see page 270)—approached them about master planning the conversion of Vanderbilt's Peabody College into a new freshman campus. At the same time, Ms. Ingram and then chancellor, Nicholas Zeppos, wanted to provide the rest of the student body with a similar integrated learning and living environment. They decided to install a residential college system, and the firm developed a master plan for renovating and building new buildings on the main campus to house 4,800 students in residential colleges. Mr. Zeppos saw residential colleges as the means to create "citizen-scholars." In 2013, after learning it would cost over $25 million to renovate the 1960s-era, high-rise Carmichael dormitories, which were highly undesirable, Mr. Zeppos decided to move forward with the residential college master plan. When he asked Ms. Ingram, who by then had stepped down as chairperson, to spearhead the effort for the remainder of the colleges, she agreed with the strong suggestion that the Schwarz team be hired as design architects. Subsequently, they hired the firm for master planning and building design of what became the four West End residential colleges.

E. Bronson Ingram College (EBI) was the first of the firm's four buildings and the site was chosen because it didn't require demolishing the high-rise dorms. Design and construction phasing were like a giant shell game, needing to make sure the university always had sufficient beds. As with the firm's work in New Haven (see page 210) and Spartanburg (see page 222), they chose a collegiate Gothic vocabulary, based on its centuries of association with quality education. The clients and design team visited the residential colleges at Yale, Harvard, and Princeton to confirm this choice. Consistent with the clients' preference, the firm's Vanderbilt designs are a more straightforward interpretation of collegiate Gothic than their more stylized work at Yale and USC Upstate. All the colleges feature both public and more private, student-only courtyards and connecting paths.

EBI is designed to relate to two of Vanderbilt's most historic buildings, Kirkland Hall, a Victorian Gothic building and Alumni Hall, a classic collegiate Gothic building. At the same time, the university's desire to maintain one of Vanderbilt's historic gingko trees required the building to be set back at a place where a natural transition in the architectural style could occur. The east side of the building, facing the main formal entrance of the campus, is composed of dark red molded bricks with red, Indian sandstone details and double-hung windows, based on the context of Kirkland Hall; the west side of the building, facing Alumni Lawn where graduation is held, is designed to complement Alumni Hall with a mix of variegated brick, Indiana limestone, Tennessee Crab Orchard sandstone, and steel casement windows. Features include dormers, chimneys (hiding mechanical, electrical and plumbing equipment), corbelled brickwork, metal gates, arched windows, towers, bays, oriels, arcades, and vaulted entries.

ARS LONGA

page 228: Entry to E. Bronson Ingram College
preceding: Façade and tower
opposite: View from courtyard
left and below: Varying aesthetic expressions break down the college's mass

E.BRONSON
INGRAM

opposite, clockwise from top left: Entry portal; Arcade; Double-height window; Dining hall
top: View into courtyard
bottom: Common room
following: E. Bronson Ingram College tower

EMERGENCY
EMERGENCY

The firm's second college, named after Chancellor Zeppos, is located at the very northwestern corner of campus and is the first building one sees approaching the campus from the west. While the program for this college is largely the same as for EBI, the site is smaller and required a denser solution, so there is one less courtyard and more floors. The architects took great care to design the building so that the bars of residential space on the south sides of the courtyards were lower, allowing plenty of natural light into these spaces. Zeppos incorporates a 310-foot-high Gothic tower into the college. This structure marks Vanderbilt on Nashville's rising skyline—the tower is clearly visible from downtown—and it houses apartments for visiting scholars and several large conference rooms on its four top floors.

The use of materials and juxtaposition of features vary from college to college, both for variety and to give each a greater individuality and sense of place. It also makes the complex appear to have been built over a greater time span. Variations include many different types of bricks, the ratio of brick to stone, the types of stone, how the stone is utilized, and the brick patterns.

The university and the architects agreed that first and foremost, the residential colleges should encourage student interaction. The program was developed based on that goal: each college contains a suite of unique and highly articulated spaces including a dining room, a servery, a great room, and classrooms that are open to everyone on campus. Student rooms and their supporting spaces, like study rooms, lounges, and bathrooms, are located behind a secure lobby and arranged around a series of light-filled green courtyards. Generous stairways are located at key points in the courtyards to encourage students to use the courtyards. Corridors serving the student rooms are designed to be short in length to encourage smaller groups of students to develop community. Each college is designed with a unique set of interior finishes to help create a distinctive identity. In EBI, mahogany wall paneling, cherry and terrazzo floors, and a three-story vaulted dining-room ceiling create that college's character, while in Zeppos College, walnut paneling, Crab Orchard sandstone and porcelain tile floors, and a white subway tile in the servery give that college its unique charm.

To further strengthen each college's unique flavor, in addition to each creating a community of 300 scholars, they each have one exclusive program element: a dance studio at EBI, the tower at Zeppos College, and a black-box and multipurpose event space at the remaining two residential colleges.

As of this book's publication, the first two colleges are finished; the third, Rothschild College, was only just finished; and the fourth began construction in the autumn of 2021.

top: Zeppos residential college from West End Avenue
opposite: Entry and tower beyond
following: Brick and stone façade details

preceding: Bay window into common room
opposite: Portal opening to courtyard
this page: Courtyard views

clockwise from top left: Courtyard arcade; Servery adjoining dining hall; Alcove; Double-height common room; Main lobby
following: Dining hall with fan-vaulted ceiling

opposite: Zeppos College tower detail
top left: Seminar room in tower; **top right:** Typical apartment
bottom: Tower lobby
following: Paneled events space atop tower

CULTURAL

NANCY LEE AND PERRY R. BASS PERFORMANCE HALL

Fort Worth, Texas, 1998
Client: Performing Arts Fort Worth

David M. Schwarz Architects' work on the Nancy Lee and Perry R. Bass Performance Hall—or Bass Hall, as it is more commonly known—began as an outgrowth of the firm's master planning efforts for the Bass family in the Sundance Square neighborhood of Downtown Fort Worth, Texas. The firm's first task was to help select the appropriate site from the family's land holdings of nearly thirty square blocks. As multipurpose theaters have a stagehouse with a very wide and high exterior wall, the project team decided to utilize a site on the periphery of those land holdings. The team selected a site where they knew a neighboring property owner planned an eleven-story garage on the adjacent site to the south. Furthermore, the family controlled the block to the east. This adjacent block would become the site for the Maddox Muse Center, Bass Hall's office, rehearsal, recital, and banquet facility, also designed by the Schwarz team. Furthermore, it allowed noisy, head-end, mechanical equipment to occupy a basement level below the street between the two blocks, as well as a portion of the Maddox Muse Center, with a façade that indeed looks like a mechanical building.

Fort Worth has small downtown block sizes. The limited area posed a significant challenge in fitting the entire program for this 2,100-seat multiuse theater onto one block. The program had been determined years before during extended discussions among the future resident companies. The client group did not wish to reopen that process. It was the architect's solution to this design challenge that led the client group to hire them as design architects for the project.

The small site presented another challenge for which the architects had a highly unique solution. For acoustic isolation reasons, the plan developed with two large mechanical ducts just inboard of the front façade. Rather than having large areas of windowless, unembellished limestone, the architects elected to place two angels—artist-designed and carved, 48-foot-high, limestone angels, weighing approximately 150 tons each—in front of those ducts. Why angels? In Greek, the word "angelos" means "messenger of the gods." One of their purposes was to bring divine inspiration to humankind and give people the inspiration for all arts. Thus, the heralding angels, with their trumpets, bring many forms of art to the citizens of Fort Worth.

The client group initially assumed the hall would be classical in style to reference the repertoire performed therein. However, complex design parameters including the section of the auditorium seating tiers and the need for barrier-free access to all levels led to a discontinuity of lobby levels across the principal façades. The architects' early studies proved classic façade options to be quite unsuccessful. Instead, they turned to what they deemed a neo-secessionist approach, which freed them from the rigors of classical design—just as the original Viennese secessionists had freed themselves from the strict neoclassicism of their time. The architects further employed this aesthetic in the interior public spaces and the Founders Concert Theater, where they used the angel motif for some of the iconographic architectural detailing. Decorative murals depicting Texas flora and fauna embellish many ceilings throughout the interiors, save for

the concert-theater ceiling, where a trompe l'oeil skylight and surrounding angel feathers adorn the acoustically diffusive central dome. Patrons can also find the feather motif cast into the seat-end stanchions, etched into the elevator doors, and laid up as herringbone veneers on wood paneling.

The concert theater is a modified opera-house form with stacked, horseshoe-shaped seating tiers (orchestra, parterre, box, mezzanine, and lower and upper galleries), with vertically aligned parapet fronts. The architects included four singular features, projecting "piano boxes" on each side of each gallery level. They also borrowed from their sports-facilities experience to add features—somewhat unique for the time in performing-arts venues, but now commonplace—that increased not only ancillary income for the facility, but also patron amenities and donor appeal. Bass Hall features private anterooms as entries to the boxes. The Founders Lounge and green room provide additional prestige for box-tier patrons. The team added catering support at every lobby level, a gift shop, and many forms of donor recognition to the program to attract donors and support supplementary income generation. Donors fully supported the cost of all original program items before the ground breaking, thus allowing the addition of many upgrades as fundraising continued. These included embellishments to the orchestra shell, Founders-room finishes, and light fixtures, as well as the incorporation of the decorative murals.

page 256: Sculpted limestone angels
above: East Fourth Street façade and primary entrance
opposite: Lobby details

"There is no question that over the past ten years, the number of restaurants in Sundance Square and the sales from those restaurants has increased anually by double digits, and clearly Bass has played a huge part."

—Tracy Gilmour

Director of Marketing, Sundance Square

top (left and right): Patron lounge
left: Proscenium set with orchestra shell
above: Auditorium details
opposite: View from stage

STEINWAY & SONS

SEVERANCE HALL

Cleveland, Ohio, 1998
Client: Musical Arts Association

When John Severance, an executive with John D. Rockefeller's Standard Oil of Ohio and a founder of several other Cleveland-based industries, became president of the Musical Arts Association, he became instrumental in building a new dedicated home for the fledgling Cleveland Orchestra. Constructed between 1929 and 1931 on the edge of Case Western Reserve University's campus, Severance Hall became a de facto memorial to Mr. Severance's wife, Elisabeth, when she passed away from a stroke shortly after his initial million-dollar contribution in 1928. Despite the stock market crash of 1929, Mr. Severance's gifts ballooned to over $2.5 million dollars, in order to ensure completion of this edifice.

As the orchestra grew in quality and prestige—becoming the youngest orchestra to achieve top-five status in America as well as gaining an international reputation—Severance Hall had a less glorious history in the second half of the twentieth century. Although it was a beloved local landmark, designed by the noted Cleveland architectural firm of Walker & Weeks, Severance Hall was never fully renovated and suffered from several inappropriate functional interventions over the decades—including a new women's dressing room that blocked half the ground-floor circulation, and the filling in of the original drive-through drop-off with a dimly lit restaurant that blocked access to two of the four grand staircases leading to the grand foyer. The final drawback came in the 1990s, when Case Western Reserve University built the new Western Plaza above a new 300-car, below-grade garage, which they made available to orchestra patrons on event nights. What was originally a chauffers' entry on one side of the rear façade became the most used public entrance. It led patrons down a rabbit warren–like path to the aforementioned, compromised drive-through space.

While solving the public circulation issues was perhaps the most pressing need, it was a musical issue that jump-started the project. Severance Hall was originally built for both symphonic and operatic performances. A 6,025-pipe Skinner Organ was placed in a loft above the stagehouse, and it was supposed to play through a "tone chute" in the hall's ceiling. It never worked well, and in 1958 the legendary music director George Szell entombed it in the attic when he added a fixed orchestra shell on the stage. In the years prior to the renovation, then music director Christoph von Dohnányi insisted that the organ be made useable again, so he could expand the orchestra's repertoire. Thus, the project was launched.

After a two-stage, by-invitation selection process, the Musical Arts Association retained David M. Schwarz Architects in 1997 to address the above problems and many others. Indeed, it was not a single project, but many smaller ones. The major design challenge was knitting these into a coherent whole that respected the historic fabric and Walker & Weeks's design intent. All in, the project entailed approximately 120,000 square feet of work: one-third new construction, one-third historic restoration, and one-third adaptive repurposing of space within the existing building. Every operational aspect of the building and orchestra was touched—from loading, back-of-house, food service, and retail, to the arrival

sequence of patrons, donor amenity areas, barrier-free seating, and the concert platform.

The addition was too small for the architects to feel comfortable making any new architectural statement in contrast with the building's historic aesthetic. As such, they decided to rely strongly on existing materials, rhythms, and detailing for design clues. New limestone came from the same quarry as the original, and the expanded street façades and outer portion of the new back façade replicated the typical bays of the existing façades. Only subtle clues separate the new from the old. For the center portion of the addition, the Schwarz team designed a new plaza façade to address the university. Its new pilasters, similar to existing ones, are adorned with a new Severance Order Ionic capital with inverted treble-clef volutes, grapes ornamenting the echinus, and an organ keyboard replacing standard egg and dart motifs. As only back-of-house spaces were behind this elevation, no doors were provided. However, a below-grade portion of the addition provides a new entry for those parking in the garage, leading directly to a new rear lobby. The relocated organ occupies the new section above the ground level.

Inside, two structural columns were relocated to accommodate two new, symmetrically placed corridors, which flank the chamber hall. These corridors are lined with a new restaurant and other patron amenities, and they connect the rear lobby to a new lobby in the old drive-through space, where the old restaurant was. Ample restrooms were added forward of this lobby. One flight up, the grand foyer was restored to its former, original splendor. Perhaps nowhere was the renovation more noteworthy than in the transformation of the auditorium itself. The aluminum leaf and pastiglia (three-dimensional plasterwork) were fully restored, as was the woodwork and decorative painting. The team removed the shell added by George Szell and replaced it with a new, stylistically compatible concert platform. The original proscenium arch, covered by Szell, was revealed and restored. The room's form was originally a modified majestic theater; with the new platform and restored proscenium, it now reads as a concert hall with the orchestra playing in a large alcove integrated with the room. While there never was a true concert platform before, the architects used an old drawing of a moveable backdrop for design inspiration. They asked, "What would Walker & Weeks have done if faced with the same challenge?" In addition, the relocated Skinner organ now plays through a new acoustically transparent, Schwarz-designed organ façade along the upstage wall of the platform.

page 262: New orchestra shell detail
above: Expanded rear façade
opposite (top): Enhanced patron entry sequence;
(bottom): Severance Restaurant

"The architects absolutely understood how patrons move in a performance and sports facility where people aren't moving all the time but at very particular points in time. They need to get in and out and have the services they need at intermission."

—Thomas Morris

Executive Director, Cleveland Orchestra

top: Restored lobby detail
bottom: Restored Reinberger Chamber Hall
opposite: Restored lobby
following: Auditorium with new orchestra shell

SCHERMERHORN SYMPHONY CENTER

Nashville, Tennesee, 2006
Client: The Nashville Symphony

The city of Nashville has two well-known monikers: Music City USA and The Athens of the South. For the leadership of the Nashville Symphony Orchestra, it was paramount that when people thought of the first, they were not just thinking of country music. As for the second, it was bestowed not because Nashville has the only full-scale replica of the Parthenon; it is because of the many institutions of higher learning within the city. These factors, and the fact that the symphony's repertoire is predominantly classical music, led the leadership to a strong predisposition for a new classical concert hall. In fact, during the building committee's kickoff meeting with David M. Schwarz Architects, the committee chairman took the architect's project manager to a window overlooking Centennial Park. Pointing to the Parthenon replica, he said, "If you make it look like that, we will all be happy."

It was a nice start, but to the Schwarz team, it was also important that the building be of its time and place, rather than merely copying past classical or neoclassical designs. Their goal was a twenty-first-century, reinterpreted classicism, that would be both timeless and appropriate for Nashville and its symphony, which was swiftly gaining national recognition. Another of the stakeholder group's strong predispositions was that the "front" should face a brand-new civic park, which unfortunately meant it would also face the ramp to parking below the park. For this reason and others, which the firm discussed with the group, it was eventually decided to have the ceremonial front, with its pedimented portico, face north and create a pedestrian-only street named Symphony Place. In fact, the building has many fronts, and the architects placed a colonnaded garden court opposite the park, making it not unlike New York's Frick Museum and its relationship to Fifth Avenue.

As with all its projects, the firm carefully studied the city's rich architectural history and eventually focused on an array of churches. One in particular caught their attention—the William Strickland-designed Downtown Presbyterian Church. The front columns and entablature, erected in 1871, had a distinctive Egyptian flair. In fact, the entablature had a symbol of Ra the sun god. Paying homage to this local landmark seemed like an appropriate point of departure from academic classicism for achieving the team's stylistic intentions. Thus, the Schermerhorn's detailing employs many Egyptian-influenced elements, including column proportions, their capitals, the entablatures, and cornices—all with gentle curves. The various limestone textures and the way the window heads, sills, and jambs are detailed, is a subtle yet visible indication that the Schermerhorn isn't strictly classical. Lastly, the ratio of solid exterior wall to windows and door openings certainly is not classical. This proportion is more akin to Karl Friedrich Schinkel's opera house in Berlin than a Renaissance building. There is a lot more glass than in a classical building, so the patrons inside can see outside, and from the outside, passersby can see the activity inside.

As part of the project's early planning the architects, acousticians, and theater planners took the client group on a European concert-hall tour. Most had classic, shoebox-form rooms—just as the Schermerhorn ultimately did—but they also visited the early 1960s Berliner Philharmonie,

a "vineyard-style" room, as a counterpoint. The team liberally borrowed some of the finest venue characteristics that they saw. The arrangement of lobby spaces around the auditorium and the back-of-house layout were reminiscent of the Concertgebouw in Amsterdam. The natural light in the auditorium was a feature of the Musikveriensaal in Vienna and the Tonhalle in Zurich. The most challenging lesson from the tour was the flat orchestra-level floor. While common in many venues in Europe, these would be unacceptable to American audiences. However, the client saw an ancillary income opportunity of being able to rent a room that size with a flat floor. Over halfway through schematic design, the client asked for a flat floor. The solution was a mechanized convertible floor. These had been used before on a limited basis in smaller recital halls, but never in a large concert hall. The team developed a scheme whereby stagehands can use a forestage lift and seven massive chair wagons, stretching from the parterre on one side to the opposite-side parterre to switch from raked concert seating to a flat parquet floor in less than an hour. In addition to room rentals, the orchestra also deploys the flat floor for jazz concerts and cabaret-style symphony pops concerts.

In addition to the architect's frequent use of locally inspired iconographic images for interior and exterior ornament, they also incorporated several pieces of commissioned artwork. The iconography includes many forms of irises, passion flowers, sugar cubes, coffee beans, and steamboat pilot wheels to name a handful. Additionally, the architects modified the church's Ra symbol into the "flying lyre" motif, which they executed in limestone on the façades and metalwork on the organ case. The concert hall's color scheme was the favorite color of the symphony's board chairperson, and the sugar cubes were a nod to the symphony's CEO and president, who liked all things sweet. The outdoor art includes *The Birth of Apollo,* a sculpture by Casey Eskridge, in the main fountain and the *Recording Angel* sculpture by Audrey Flack in a plaza south of the stage door. Most impressive is the 48-foot-wide and 12-foot-tall haute-relief limestone sculpture by Raymond Kaskey on the north pediment that depicts *Orpheus and Euridice,* the myth from which came the saying, "Music soothed the savage beast."

page 270: Lobby stair detail
above: Symphony Place façade
opposite (top): Fourth Avenue South façade; **(bottom):** Fountain at corner of Symphony Place and Fourth Avenue South
following (left): Main lobby; **(right):** East lobby

"Music City USA ain't all fiddling and sipping whiskey no more."

—Professor Michael Linton

School of Music, Middle Tennessee State University

clockwise from top left: East lobby concessions; East lobby detail; Green room; Balcony lobby
opposite: Founders room
following (left): Concert platform from Founders tier boxes
(right): Auditorium from concert platform
pages 280–281: Laura Turner Hall

THE PALLADIUM

Carmel, Indiana, 2010
Client: Carmel Redevelopment Commission

The Palladium, the largest hall and center point of the Center for the Performing Arts in Carmel, Indiana was the longtime dream of long-serving Mayor James Brainard. Carmel is an exurban community contiguous with Indianapolis's northern boundary. While adjacent, downtown Indianapolis is still forty-five minutes away by car. Mayor Brainard wanted Carmel to be more than a bedroom community for Indianapolis. He wanted a vibrant community with a mix of housing types, community-serving retail, employment opportunities, restaurants, and nightlife. He put in place many zoning, subdivision, and transportation initiatives that made Carmel innovative and more attractive. Carmel became the roundabout capital of the western hemisphere and has two highly regarded New Urbanist developments. However, a city center and cultural offerings were still missing. So, under the auspices of the Carmel Redevelopment Commission, he launched the Center for the Performing Arts and commissioned David M. Schwarz Architects to design the Palladium, a 1,600-seat concert hall with accommodations for various types of artistic performances.

The chosen site was four-sided. To the north was a major new east–west connector street; to the west was Third Avenue, which provided vehicular access; to the south was the planned new Village Green; and to the east was City Center, a mixed-use development, whose first phase was then under construction. A four-sided building was in order. The main ceremonial front would face the Village Green. Patron drop-off and the box office would address Third Avenue. Another entry to the east fronted the Monon Trail, a rails-to-trail pathway between the Palladium site and City Center. The back-of-house faced the north. Even without an entrance or street access, the back-of-house needed to be the fourth primary façade. David Schwarz had always been intrigued by the numerous forms of symmetry: reflectional, bilateral, rotational, and radial to name a handful. Renaissance architect Andrea Palladio's Villa Rotunda in northern Italy exhibited many of these forms, and thus, albeit smaller in scale, it became the archetype for the Palladium's massing. The Palladium therefore became one of a long line of similar buildings starting with Villa Rotunda, through Henbury Hall in Cheshire, Mereworth Castle in Kent, and the Lowe Library at Columbia University.

While the massing is the same on all four sides and all four corners, the architects varied the fenestration and detailing of each face to address location and function. The south façade has a ceremonial staircase leading to a raised portico with giant order columns and pediment. East and west entries feature inset, ground-level porticos under projecting balconies with single-story columns. As Indiana is known for its fine limestone—quarried a mere two-hour drive south of Carmel—the mayor wanted a limestone building. Concerns about the budget led the architects to submit two schematic design options: one all limestone in neo-successionist, stylized classicism, and the other using Romanesque brickwork with limestone details. However, the firm did not know that countless high school gymnasiums throughout Indiana were constructed of brick and limestone in a Romanesque style. The mayor chose the limestone design.

To offset the cost of the limestone on the exterior, the interiors had to be elegant yet very cost-efficient. Rather than layering on three-dimensional ornament and detail, the Schwarz team turned to polychromatic paint schemes for much of said detail and ornament. They drew inspiration from the Adams Style (also known as Adamesque), the work of eighteenth-century Scottish neoclassicists, the Adam Brothers. The firm continued this stylistic approach into the concert hall itself, while adding three-dimensional relief for acoustic reasons. Symmetry played a major role here as well. The room is composed of a central volume, which is bilaterally symmetrical side to side and, more unusually, front to back. It is topped with an oval dome with an oculus at its apex, providing natural light into the audience chamber. Forward and back from the central volume, the room extends into two alcoves, which are identical in volume and are both topped with matching half domes. They differ only in that the upstage one houses the concert platform and organ façade while the back one houses the rear parterre an additional, raised seating level.

The largest challenge for the architects was working for the first time with an acoustic consulting firm with widely differing concepts for acoustics, space, and design. They required a large, solid, forestage canopy reaching far downstage into the room. This would have blocked most views to the domes, and applying Adamesque detailing to a solid object that large would have been contrary to the historic precedence and otherwise inappropriate for the design. The architects' counter proposal was to utilize a transparent, glass canopy comprising many sizes and shapes of glass "shards" suspended from traveling spaceframes. The thinking was that this concept would preserve the read of the room and views to the dome, while meeting the acousticians' design criteria. They concurred, and the design team worked collaboratively to bring this innovative and unique design to fruition.

page 282: Corner detail
preceding: Primary entry on Third Avenue SW
above: South lobby
opposite (clockwise from top left): Concessions detail; Balcony lobby; West lobby from balcony; Donors' lounge suite

top: Auditorium west wall
bottom: Auditorium from concert platform
opposite: Concert platform from orchestra level

THE SMITH CENTER FOR THE PERFORMING ARTS

Las Vegas, Nevada, 2012
Client: Las Vegas Performing Arts Center Foundation

From its inception, the developers of the Smith Center for the Performing Arts saw it as becoming the cultural anchor of the 64-acre redevelopment of the Union Pacific rail yards immediately east of downtown Las Vegas. In fact, they imagined it as a cultural destination for the entire Las Vegas region for residents and visitors alike. As such, the client group had one paramount instruction for architects: the Smith Center had to be authentic and timeless. However, determining what authentic and timeless meant to Las Vegas was no easy task for David M. Schwarz Architects. In a region with ersatz everything—from New York, to Paris, to Egypt, Rome, Lake Como, and everything in between—and where a building's life span is measured in decades, not centuries, what was authentic and what would stand the test of time? Fortunately, the answer was massive, nearly a hundred years old, and only 25 miles away as the crow flies: the Hoover Dam. With the dam in mind, the architects employed a bold American art deco–inspired design aesthetic that paid homage to this iconic structure. Moreover, unlike the ersatz pretenders, the Smith Center uses materials that are just what they appear to be: limestone and stainless steel on the exterior and marble, granite, Venetian plaster, and hardwood on the interior.

The Donald W. Reynolds Foundation (headquartered in Las Vegas), chief benefactor of the center, wanted to be able to see all three major parts of the program for the project from the new Symphony Park, a central green space in the rail yards redevelopment. This goal led to a master-plan solution that configured the program in three distinct buildings around an internal pedestrian way—in the same manner as Schubert Alley on Broadway—leading to a palm-lined courtyard. To the east is the principal performance space, Reynolds Hall, a 2,100-seat, multipurpose theater in a modified opera-house form. A second structure to the west, of matching limestone and detailing, the Boman Pavilion, houses Myron's Cabaret Jazz, the flexible Troesh Studio rehearsal hall, and the Wynn Studio for Arts Education. Both Reynolds Hall and the Boman Pavilion have predominately symmetrical façades, save for the Reynolds Halls east tower, and each building has one curved corner inflecting to the pedestrian promenade and courtyard. At the south side of the courtyard a third, limestone-clad building was changed from an originally programmed smaller hall to a new home for the Discovery Children's Museum. The museum wanted a separate street presence and image, so the Schwarz team reinterpreted the Smith Center detailing in a palette of herringbone-patterned brick and limestone with a large semicircular window flanked by two deco bays.

At the direct request of the client group, Reynolds Hall, unlike many of the firm's performance venues, has a very large, central lobby on the orchestra level, capable of holding the majority of the patrons. The architects did not stop there. They designed the interior circulation to be part of the act, experiencing spatial compression and expansion along the way from the street to the performance hall. Las Vegas is very much a see-and-be-seen town. Patrons enter one of two corner entrance foyers, which lead to the grand lobby with generous natural light, a mix of red and gray marbles, and stainless-steel details. Vertical circulation, using a series of interconnecting

spaces, encourage patrons to use the stairs to get to their seats. At the mezzanine level, three distinctively designed lounges provide private box and dress-circle ticket holders with more intimate gathering spaces. The main staircase culminates at the balcony level with another large lobby and outdoor terrace. Patrons enter a soaring five-tiered performance hall crowned with a large multitiered light fixture. Reynolds Hall is a multipurpose room and the architects, assisted by the acousticians, designed its interior architecture to work seamlessly with the acoustic flexibility the room demands.

While verticality dominates the design of Reynolds Hall, horizontality figures prominently in the lobbies and circulation of the Boman Pavilion. The architects used Venetian plaster on the walls (a more affordable solution here than the marble used in Reynolds Hall) with aluminum reveals, custom painted friezes, cove light fixtures, and stainless-steel railings, all contributing to an attractive, cost-effective mix of materials. Here again, the design team's focus for lobbies, circulation, and performance spaces is the experience of seeing other people.

The designers added many signature elements to give the Smith Center an iconic stature throughout the region. Foremost is the 170-foot-tall tower with its stainless-steel pinnacle, which houses a four-octave carillon utilizing forty-seven real, bronze bells, rather than recorded music. A casting of a *Winged Figure of the Republic,* as seen at the Hoover Dam, presides over the grand lobby in Reynolds Hall. It occupies the first landing of the symmetrical grand staircase with cascading stainless-steel railings. In the hall itself, the acoustically diffusive octagonal, stepped dome provides a central focus to the ceiling, and an acoustically transonic, stainless-steel proscenium frames the stage. Behind the stage at Cabaret Jazz a glass wall overlooks Symphony Park. Cabaret Jazz also features a hanging mezzanine, which allows for a clear main floor uninterrupted by columns. In addition, throughout public and donor spaces, custom furniture—designed by the architects—complements the art deco details. The architects also used iconography throughout the buildings to reinforce their uses and location, including piano shapes in the return air grills and mountain motifs for the interior friezes of the theater. These mountain motifs also appear in exterior work and stainless-steel panels.

page 290: Benjamin Victor's *Genius in Flight* on grand staircase
above: Symphony Park façade
opposite (clockwise from top left): Court between Reynolds Hall and the Boman Pavilion; Bas-relief panel; View across Symphony Park
following: Reynolds Hall main lobby

RIGHT
BOX TIER

FOUNDERS ROOM

"Reynolds Hall is acoustically a first-rate hall, and architecturally a first-rate hall. That's a rare, rare achievement. We were thrilled to play there."

—Garry Hanson
Executive Director, The Cleveland Orchestra

clockwise from top left: Main stair gallery; Oculus over upper-level main staircase; Founders room; Box tier foyer
opposite: Auditorium view from stage
following: Stage view from box tier

clockwise from top: Upper lobby; View into lobby; Air-return grille detail; Lighting detail
opposite (top): Troesch Studio Theater; **(bottom):** Cabaret Jazz Theater

CABARET JAZZ
A CLUB AT THE SMITH CENTER
CABARET JAZZ

GAILLARD

CHARLESTON GAILLARD CENTER

Charleston, South Carolina, 2015
Client: City of Charleston

The Gaillard Municipal Auditorium and Exhibit Hall in Charleston, South Carolina opened in 1968. It served Charleston's needs when it launched, but by 1977—when the Spoleto Festival USA had commenced and the Gaillard Center had become the multivenue festival's largest hall—its many drawbacks became apparent. Its compromised acoustics were not equal to the demands of the festival's international exposure. The seat count was too large for many events, yet the other venues were too small. It was also too large for most locally produced events. The room's extremely large, single balcony made a sizeable portion of the orchestra-level seats, below it, undesirable. Lastly, its aesthetics—never compatible with the Charleston peninsula's historic character—and its modest materials were already outdated.

However, two factors prevented construction of a replacement on the peninsula. First, changes in the zoning regulation for the historic district would not allow sufficient height for a fly tower. Second, the Federal Emergency Management Agency's mapping of the hundred-year hurricane storm surge would not allow construction of a new orchestra pit. Over the next few decades, several studies for renovations and replacement produced no results.

By 2008, Charleston native Martha Rivers Ingram, then chairperson of the Spoleto Festival USA's board, decided to do something. At her urging, Spoleto Festival USA retained David M. Schwarz Architects—with whom she had worked in Nashville—to prepare a program and concept design for the renovation of the complex. After completing the study at the end of that year, Ms. Ingram began friendly discussions with Charleston's longtime mayor, Joseph Riley, about a public-private partnership to implement the architect's plan. Slightly more than a year later, Mayor Riley determined a method for the city to fund its half of the cost. The project's program would have to include 80,000 square feet of municipal offices and the conversion of the exhibit hall into an expanded banquet and meeting facility. With these changes, the project was relaunched.

In addition to the Gaillard's problems discussed, its site was a superblock created when the city demolished four adjacent blocks and vacated the streets in between. The original architects placed the structure within the middle of the new superblock, removed from any street, in a most un-Charleston-like manner. A nondescript parking garage and county school-board office building were later additions to the block. To rectify this unfortunate condition, the architects placed most of the new office space to the south of the existing building, bringing the structure's relationship to the streetscape in line with the rest of George Street. A half-oval entry court marks the entry to the building's shared lobby, "the Galleria." On the west side, the architects arranged more of the office program, the new loading dock, and a new service corridor—which reads as an enclosed porch—in a stepping fashion along the slanted Anson Street, relating to the streetscape in the same manner as the church, parish house, and elementary school across the street. To the north, they extended the banquet facility and completely redesigned the public green space on Calhoun Street, taking what had been

a large, undifferentiated lawn and transforming it into a series of well-defined and landscaped outdoor rooms, worthy of the city's heritage of fine gardens. They used four small stucco pavilions to frame the north entrance plaza. Equally important, the firm employed a series of circular and oval geometries in their design of both the Galleria and landscape, which creates a pedestrian path—inside and out—where the original, north–south street once ran.

The architects also employed other curvilinear geometries throughout the building's exterior and interior. As Charleston was originally a French community, the Schwarz team adopted a French late-Renaissance aesthetic with baroque-like touches. Executed in variegated Indiana limestone and a lime-based stucco, these design features, large and small, included the entry court discussed above, curving pedimented porticos at both main entries, filleted corners on towers and bay elements, and crescent-shaped haunches at the tower tops. They also incorporated specific Charleston iconographic symbols, such as the crescent, palmetto trees, Gullah weavings, and the yellow jessamine flower, into their stylized, beaked-Ionic, "Gaillard Order" column capitals, used both on the exterior and interior. Inside, the architects used curvilinear forms for terrazzo patterns, railings, floor openings, the auditorium's seating tiers, and several intricate, vaulted ceilings. The new auditorium—Rivers Performance Hall, named after Ms. Ingram's parents—is a modified opera-house form crowned with a multitiered, ribbed ceiling dome, which the architects aligned vertically with each seating tiers' parapet fronts below. Each of the center's primary public areas employs a unique color scheme, with off-white trim unifying the different palettes. All feel very Southern. For the auditorium, Ms. Ingram and the architects selected apricot. Its lobbies are beige. The Galleria is celadon, the same color scheme Ms. Ingram requested for Laura Turner Hall at the Schermerhorn Symphony Center (see page 270). Lastly, the banquet and meeting rooms are a Wedgewood-like blue-gray. This suite of rooms consists of a large subdividable ballroom with pre-function spaces on the street level, and more pre-function spaces and meeting rooms one level above.

The newly renamed Charleston Gaillard Center reopened on October 9, 2015, with world-renowned cellist Yo-Yo Ma and the Charleston Symphony playing for the grand gala's patrons. For the first season of the Spoleto Festival in the new facility in the spring of 2016, Rivers Performance Hall hosted a stunning rendition of *Porgy and Bess,* the great Gershwin opera set in Charleston, making a fitting tribute to the city and its culture.

page 302: Pediment detail
preceding and opposite: George Street entrance
above (left): Corner with neighboring context; **(right):** Seating tiers on Anson Street

clockwise from top left: Rivers Hall orchestra-level lobby; Rivers Hall lobby stairs; Common lobby stairs, north; Common lobby stairs, south
opposite (top): Gallery-level lobby; **(bottom):** Founders room
following: Rivers Performance Hall

CHAPMAN CULTURAL CENTER

Spartanburg, South Carolina, 2007
Client: The Arts Partnership of Greater Spartanburg

Founded in the 1950s, the Arts Council of Spartanburg—renamed the Arts Partnership of Greater Spartanburg in the 1990s and now simply referred to as the Chapman Cultural Center—is an alliance of several arts institutions in the greater Spartanburg, South Carolina area. It includes children's and community theater, history and art museums, a ballet and associated school, a science center, and an artists' guild. In the year 2000, they kicked off a campaign to build a combined facility to increase synergy between these groups. Unfortunately, their first design proved to be irreconcilably over-budget, which caused a pause in their efforts.

The construction manager for that endeavor had worked with David M. Schwarz Architects on many prior projects including Bass Hall in Fort Worth, Texas (see page 256). They were well aware of the firm's perfect record of delivering performing-arts venues on time and within budget. After the Schwarz team was introduced to the various arts institutions, work recommenced with a new design lead. The first move by the new architects was to separate the acoustically critical theater uses from the remainder of the program. This move to divide the complex into three distinct buildings allowed the theater building to have a load-bearing masonry and steel structure, and the other two to be of less costly, bar joist construction. Additionally, the team remotely located noisy mechanical equipment in the other two buildings.

The central building houses a multipurpose lobby/meeting room/event space and a 500-seat proscenium theater for use by local theater groups; however, with a full-size fly tower, it is also suitable as a roadhouse for any traveling production that plays to a 500-seat house. This structure is set back from the street, which provides an entry court for all three buildings. The exterior is beige limestone in stylized Greek Revival classicism. A three-bay, giant order portico with double outer columns leads to the central lobby and provides the ceremonial front to the complex. At each side, curving, one-story colonnades connect the center building to the flanking buildings. Those buildings, each two stories, are clad in a rich, medium red brick with limestone details and accents, which visually reference back to the center building. The architects placed these building along the sidewalk to reinforce the streetscape. Their entries, within wide, two-story, limestone-framed arched openings, oppose each other across the entry court. Narrower two-story arched openings with metal spandrel panels present an even rhythm along the streetscape.

In the interior of the theater building, the architects employed terrazzo flooring and polychromatic plasterwork for ornament in several shades of Wedgewood blue-gray. The auditorium itself, with seating on a main orchestra level and smaller elevated balcony, features a ceiling with a multitiered, stepped dome, which is concentric with the parapet walls of the balcony and parterre below. The base building interiors of the flanking buildings were simple volumes that the user groups could finish out as their budgets allowed. These are extremely flexible spaces, which the Chapman Cultural Center can subdivide and adjust to address the individual space needs of the arts organizations. Additionally, the architects provided a master plan for expansion, wherein the center could add other wing buildings to the rear, should any of the organizations grow to the point of needing and being able to support their own building. The center opened in 2007, and due to the architects designing within budget—as well as the overall success of the project—by 2013, the Chapman Cultural Center was paid in full, debt-free.

page 312: Proscenium from orchestra level
opposite (top): Entrance from central plaza; **(bottom):** Enclosed central plaza
clockwise from top left: Main lobby; Spartanburg Museum of Art gallery space; Spartanburg History Museum space; Auditorium from balcony

NATIONAL COWGIRL MUSEUM AND HALL OF FAME

Fort Worth, Texas, 2002
Client: National Cowgirl Museum and Hall of Fame

When the Cowgirl Hall of Fame in Hereford, Texas, put itself up for sale, several of the most prominent and successful businesswomen of Fort Worth, Texas stepped forward. As a first step in creating a new home with more national exposure for this sleepy, local institution, this group hired David M. Schwarz Architects for preliminary planning.

Their first task was to test-fit the program in an existing building that the Modern Art Museum of Fort Worth would soon abandon. This approach proved less desirable than a new location between the Will Rogers Memorial Center and the site of a future new arena for the rodeo. The next step was a master plan for a new Western Heritage Center. The center would involve many Fort Worth institutions dedicated to the city's heritage as "Where the West Begins." These included the Museum of Science and History, the Texas and Southwestern Cattle Raisers Association Museum, an expansion of the Fort Worth Stock Show & Rodeo's livestock facilities, a new Arabian Horse Museum, and the relocated Cowgirl Hall of Fame. The project team held several stakeholder charrettes over a few months before architects produced the master plan. The plan clustered the organizations around a planned new roundabout within the Will Rogers complex, at the intersection of Burnett-Tandy Drive and Gendy Boulevard. Ultimately, the Museum of Science and History expanded, including a Cattle Raisers Museum, and the Stock Show also expanded, though plans for the Arabian Horse Museum never materialized. However, the Cowgirl Hall of Fame continued, rebranded as the National Cowgirl Museum and Hall of Fame.

The building, inspired by Fort Worth's rich history of southwestern art deco buildings, is a major element of the institution's rebranding and a signpost for itself. As such, the architects incorporated a range of iconographic elements within the façades. The museum's leadership adopted the desert rose as their primary icon: beautiful, yet tough by nature. Thus, the desert rose embellishes the center of the cast deco spandrel panels between the first and second floors. The Will Rogers complex has a long history of employing mosaics and/or glazed tiles on its building's exterior. Here, the architects used both. Polychromatic, glazed tile finials cap brick and cast stone pilasters, with stylized desert roses inset at their pinnacles. A tower element addresses the planned roundabout, the Burnett-Tandy façade is the main entry, and the architects incorporated a mosaic mural of riding cowgirls in the center of the Gendy façade. Scenes of cowgirls and ranch women appear in cast bas-relief frieze panels at the top of both primary façades. The architects used a wide-range, medium-color brick similar to the other Will Roger Memorial Center buildings; however, it was not the same. The selected brick was the only one on which the client group of strong-minded businesswomen could agree. Achieving consensus among diverse opinions has always been one of the firm's strengths.

The architects organized the interior around a central rotunda, which also serves as the actual Hall of Fame honoring the comprehensive list of inductees, from noted western figures like Annie Oakley and Sacagawea to singers like Emmylou Harris and Dale Evans, and even Supreme Court Justice Sandra Day O'Connor.

The rotunda's inner colonnade is oval, its outer walls are a stretched octagon, and it is skylit via a roof monitor. Around the second-floor balcony parapet are photo-murals of many honorees, which change—depending upon one's angle of view—by using holographs and Fresnel lenses ("wiggly-eye" technology). Between these murals are bas-relief diamonds with the desert-rose icon, and the parapets are supported by the lower colonnade with its cow-head capitals. Around the main level of the rotunda are ancillary, income-producing, front-of-house patron amenities, a flexible gallery for changing exhibits, and back-of-house spaces for conservation and loading. Around the second-level balcony are the permanent exhibits, many of them interactive.

page 316: Tower element and façade details of building at corner at Burnett-Tandy Drive and Gendy Boulevard
above: Richard Haas's trompe l'oeil mural
right (top): Ticketing desk; (**bottom**): Ground floor of rotunda
opposite: Rotunda column capital detail

SID RICHARDSON MUSEUM
SID RICHARDSON MUSEUM

SID RICHARDSON MUSEUM

Fort Worth, Texas, 2006
Client: Sid Richardson Foundation

The beginnings of the Sid Richardson Museum began with a very simple request by the executive director of the Sid Richardson Foundation, which displayed the Sid Richardson Collection of Western Art on the ground floor of its Fort Worth offices. He wanted to replace the carpeting in the offices. David M. Schwarz Architects met with him about carpet options, but the chairperson of the foundation's board had a more extensive notion; the renovation of the entire office suite and the gallery. However, reaching consensus among the full board proved more elusive than he first imagined. After a couple of false starts, an external event jump-started the project for good. While the foundation had a no-loan policy, they made an exception for the National Gallery of Art in Washington, D.C. for its exhibition *The Color of Night*. This show presented Frederic Remington's nocturne paintings, four of them from the Richardson Collection. Reframing in period frames, hanging with appropriate spacing, and illuminating with state-of-the-art lighting instruments truly transformed the appearance of these paintings. After viewing the exhibition, the foundation chairperson returned to Fort Worth with renewed desire to renovate the gallery. To ensure success, he added the National Gallery of Art's curator and exhibit designer to the project team.

The program also grew to include a complete rebranding from the Sid Richardson Collection of Western Art into the Sid Richardson Museum. For the patrons, this rebranding begins at the exterior. The building was an early-1980s reconstruction of a previously destroyed Sundance Square structure, but at the ground level the architect of the reconstruction had wanted a more modern read. Unfortunately, this design was not overly inviting to patrons or passersby. Indeed, the ground floor was solid brick, save for one pair of grey, dark, smoked-glass doors, providing no visibility into the reception and gift shop. In fact, it was almost foreboding. The Schwarz team replaced this with new clear-glass show windows between fluted red-granite columns supporting an ornamented granite entablature. The detailing makes subtle references to that of the architect's design of Tarrant County Family Law Center (see page 186). Three rows of bas-relief metal castings of the buffalo from the former United States nickel coin further adorn these columns. Additionally, the team added new signage and festive banners announcing the Sid Richardson Museum brand.

The original gallery was a single lozenge-shaped room, on a 45-degree bias, with one freestanding wall in the middle. Closely hung paintings covered the perimeter and both sides of this middle wall. Minimally functioning restrooms, vertical circulation, and a small, but income-producing gift shop, were in the four corners. The architects rearranged the entire plan. In the front, they expanded the lobby and gift shop. Behind that, they split the museum into two distinct rooms, one a six-sided gallery and the other an attenuated gallery that wraps around the former. They also designed moveable partitions, which the museum could deploy to divide each end of the attenuated gallery into smaller galleries for focused exhibitions. The National Gallery of Art's curator determined the initial installation and several future subject-matter-based exhibitions. The team chose wall colors to specifically highlight the collection. The renovation project also included modern, updated mechanical systems, fire-suppression measures, gallery lighting, security, art storage, and art-handling facilities. A new entry, information desk, and expanded gift shop are in front of the galleries, and an expansion into the building next door allows for a group entrance, fully accessible and ample restrooms, and a classroom. And, yes, they renovated the foundation's offices, and the director got new carpeting.

page 320: Storefront façade at sidewalk
clockwise from top left: Pilaster detail; View along Main Street; Gift shop
opposite: Nocturne paintings in gallery

EXIT

SELECT COMMISSIONS

2020

St. Charles Catholic Church (Arlington, Virginia) Study for the reconfiguration of a church campus adjacent to the Clarendon Metro stop, organizing sanctuary and parish house at the tip of the triangular site to address a public square, and preserving the rear of the site for development by a commercial partner.

2019

Southlake Block 20 (Southlake, Texas) Design for two four-story buildings, accommodating fifty-eight new residences with expansive living space and outdoor terraces, semiprivate elevator lobbies, and one level of below-grade parking.

St. Elmo Residential Tower Design (Bethesda, Maryland) Residential tower, twenty-two stories, 280 units, with 6,000 square feet of retail space.

Cook Children's Medical Center Dodson Specialty Clinics Expansion (Fort Worth, Texas) Medical office building, 240,000 square feet, to accommodate outpatient clinic growth.

Cook Children's Medical Center garage at 8th & Pennsylvania Avenues (Fort Worth, Texas) Parking garage (873 spots) to connect to the main campus's Dodson Specialty Clinics expansion, with upgraded valet parking zone, eight stories above-grade, and two below.

Cook Children's Medical Center Prosper Campus Design (Prosper, Texas) New community-based hospital, 213,429 square feet, five stories above-grade and one story below-grade, including a central utility plant.

2018

Duke University Residence Hall (Durham, North Carolina) Study examining the addition of a 125,000-square-foot, 365-bed dormitory to anchor the southwest corner of Duke's historic West Campus, adapting the massing, fenestration, materials, and details of the 1920s Collegiate Gothic campus.

Kennedy Center Concert Hall (Washington, D.C.) Study for renovation of the John F. Kennedy Center for the Performing Arts' 2,500-seat Concert Hall, including consideration of acoustics conditions, seating configurations, and phasing options for an improved patron experience.

MidCity Amphitheater Design (Huntsville, Alabama) Amphitheater, 8,000 seats, inspired by ancient Greek and twentieth-century precedents, including the William Randolph Hearst Greek Theatre at the University of California, Berkeley.

Riverside Master Plan (Newton, Massachusetts) Master plan to transform a 13-acre surface parking lot at a commuter rail station outside Boston into a transit-oriented mixed-use development with more than 500 residential units and over 35,000 square feet of lab, office, and retail, totaling over 1 million square feet of new construction. In association with Speck & Associates.

Sundance West Interior Renovation (Fort Worth, Texas) Redesign of Sundance West Apartments interiors, public spaces, and amenities, including proposed combination of multiple units and upgrading finishes throughout the building, to respond to evolving local market conditions.

2017

Crystal City Master Plan (Arlington, Virginia) Master plan specifying means to make the Crystal City neighborhood more pedestrian-friendly, including infilling existing deep setbacks with new retail uses, identifying sites for new mid- and high-rise buildings between Route 1 and Crystal Drive, replacing parking lots with public parks and plazas, and adding several new streets.

Cook Children's Medical Center Master Plan Update (Fort Worth, Texas) Updates to master plan for Cook Children's Medical Center, including new parking structures, improvements to main hospital entry, and expansion of the Dodson Specialty Clinics following completion of the South Tower.

Le Guanahani Restoration and Master Plan (Saint Barthélemy, French West Indies) Reconstruction plan for resort hotel following damage sustained in Hurricane Irma, including rethinking of guest rooms, suites, property circulation, food and beverage services, and improvements to restaurant, pool, oceanfront bar, and viewsheds.

New Music School, Longwood University (Farmville, Virginia) Academic building, 61,000 square feet, with concert hall, flexible recital and rehearsal spaces, classrooms, faculty studios, student practice rooms, and two-story lobby with open stairways.

Northline Master Plan (Leander, Texas) Master plan for transit-oriented development 25 miles from Austin, comprising 115 acres of walkable mixed-use development, including town square and pavilion to be surrounded by layers of commercial and residential uses.

Nicholas S. Zeppos Residential College at Vanderbilt University (Nashville, Tennessee) Second of four residential colleges to be designed for Vanderbilt University's campus, housing 340 undergraduate beds and twenty-two long-term-stay apartments for visiting scholars in a twenty-story tower.

Oak Farms Master Plan (Dallas, Texas) Master plan for redevelopment of former dairy processing plant located at a key entry point to Dallas's Oak Cliff neighborhood, integrating 5.6 million square feet of residential, hotel, office, retail, and restaurant uses into a network of streets and public squares, with an elevated promenade park overlooking the Trinity River frontage.

Seattle Arena Concept Design (Seattle, Washington) Concept studies for renovation of 18,000-seat multipurpose arena, including proposals for introducing light into lower-level concourses and improving visitor experience with enhanced circulation and wayfinding.

Southside Master Plan (Savannah, Georgia) Master plan developed as a Congress Legacy Project of the 2017 Congress for New Urbanism, envisioning a mixed-use pedestrian-oriented community and exploring potential redevelopment of the Savannah Mall.

2016

Ashview Heights Master Plan (Atlanta, Georgia) Study reimagining multiple neighborhoods in Westside, Promise Zone, including concepts for new multifamily housing and strategies for revitalizing a commercial corridor and transit station. In association with Dhiru Thadani.

The Green Ark Foundation (Santa Bárbara de Heredia, Costa Rica) Master plan and hospitality building for herb farm and botanical garden in Costa Rica, with inventive entry sequence orienting guests from a bell tower through a clerestory-lit stairway and into a dining room overlooking the farm, where concept plans propose future guest accommodations.

Private Residence (Fort Worth, Texas) Study for converting multiple units in the Sundance West Apartments building into a single-family residence with terraced gardens.

Vanderbilt University Residential Colleges (Nashville, Tennessee) Master plan for a series of residential colleges to be built at Vanderbilt University, replacing out-of-date student housing with timeless community-fostering buildings.

Wardman Park Planned Unit Development (Washington, D.C.) Study for development of hotel site adjacent to the Woodley Park Metro, to accommodate approximately 1,700 residential units.

2015

AC Hotel Spartanburg (Spartanburg, South Carolina) Hotel, 5000 square feet, 114 rooms, in downtown Spartanburg, with 5,000-square-foot rooftop bar and 2,500-square-foot meeting center.

Capital Point South (Washington, D.C.) Massing and exterior design for two buildings in three-building complex between Patterson and N Streets NE, including street and alley façades for loft-style office building at 50 Patterson and terra-cotta-clad apartment building at 51 N Street.

Chevy Chase Lake Master Plan (Chevy Chase, Maryland) Multiphase master plan for 16 acres with 500,000 square feet of new construction adjacent to the future Connecticut Avenue Purple Line light rail station, including three buildings nearing completion at time of publication, varying from six to twelve stories, with 530 residential units, 110,000 square feet of retail, public space, and three levels of underground parking.

New music school, Texas Christian University (Fort Worth, Texas) Study using a programming document designed by the university, envisioning two distinct configurations for proposed school.

Office design for the Rock Creek Group (Washington, D.C.) Reimagining of full floor of 1133 Connecticut Avenue, designed by DMSAS nearly three decades ago, as contemporary work environment for a financial firm, with transparent offices and an elliptical living room.

Parkview Residences (Southlake, Texas) First multifamily residential building approved and constructed in Southlake, consisting of thirty-six two- and three-bedroom condominium units ranging in size from 1,500 to 3,400 square feet.

Private Residence (New York, New York) Design combining two apartments into full-floor luxury residence in historic building, maximizing views of neighboring park and vibrant thoroughfare.

2014

Arlington Multifamily Residential (Arlington, Virginia) A 300,000-square-foot mixed-use apartment building offering 330 rental units with 30,000 square feet of ground-level retail.

Ballston Multifamily Residential (Arlington, Virginia) Building design for a 500,000-square-foot multifamily residential building with ground-level retail sited on 2.6 acres of under-developed land in the Ballston area of Arlington, Virginia. The building design also includes three levels of underground parking.

Cook Children's Medical Center Master Plan Update (Fort Worth, Texas) Update of the hospital's master plan, incorporating short-term planning goals as well as long-term objectives for facilities, construction, and services.

Studio Theatre (Washington, D.C.) Conceptual programmatic studies for the renovation and improvement of a four-theater complex in the Logan's Circle neighborhood of Washington, D.C.

Southlake—High Street (Southlake, Texas) Master planning and conceptual design studies for the development of additional retail and office buildings within Southlake Town Square.

Spartanburg Hotel (Spartanburg, South Carolina) Design for a new hotel sited along Main Street in downtown Spartanburg, South Carolina, featuring approximately 120 rooms and rooftop amenities.

Southlake Garden District (Southlake, Texas) Design for the second phase of Brownstone townhouses in Southlake Town Square. Exterior design will provide continuity with the original Brownstones while also offering customizable, high-end amenities. In conjunction with The Parkview apartments, this phase solidifies the new Garden District residential area within Southlake Town Square.

Vanderbilt Residential Colleges Design (Nashville, Tennessee) Programming and conceptual design for the first residential college resulting from the Residential College Master Plan.

Vanderbilt Residential College Master Plan (Nashville, Tennessee) Master-plan studies and phasing strategy development for up to nine residential colleges to house the university's 5,000 undergraduate residents.

2013

NoMa Mixed-Use Office Building (Washington, D.C.) Nine-story mixed-use office building offering 250,000 square feet of office space and 9,000 square feet of ground-level retail.

NoMa Mixed-Use Residential (Washington, D.C.) Design for mixed-use building featuring residential uses, office space, ground-level retail, and a movie theater.

The Parkview (Southlake, Texas) The first approved multifamily residential development in Southlake, this five-story building will accommodate thirty-eight units ranging from one to three bedrooms.

Plaza at Landmark (Alexandria, Virginia) Master-plan studies for the phased renovation of a 22.5-acre shopping center into a walkable mixed-use development.

Southlake Del Frisco's (Southlake, Texas) A 8,500-square-foot restaurant sited on a high-visibility corner within Southlake Town Square. The building features a demonstration kitchen, a partial second-floor dining room, and an upstairs outdoor seating terrace.

Southlake Trader Joe's (Southlake, Texas) The first grocery store in Southlake Town Square, this 13,000-square-foot grocery store is sited in close proximity to the DMSAS-designed Brownstones and The Parkview apartments.

Squirrel Island (Canada) Design for the interior and exterior renovation of a large private residence, including the main house and three large boathouses.

St. Elmo Apartments (Bethesda, Maryland) A sixteen-story apartment building accommodating approximately 200 rental apartment units, 10,000 square feet of office space and 4,000 square feet of retail space.

2012

Alpharetta City Center (Alpharetta, Georgia) Master plan for a new, 22-acre City Center in downtown Alpharetta. The plan incorporates a new City Hall, public library, private development, and open park space.

Alpharetta City Hall (Alpharetta, Georgia) Building design for a new 60,000-square-foot City Hall, which houses the Council Chambers, pre-function gathering space, much of the municipal government's departments and Alpharetta History Room. In association with Smallwood, Reynolds, Stewart, Stewart & Associates, and URS Corporation.

Cook Children's Medical Center Master Plan Update (Fort Worth, Texas) Update to the hospital's master plan, including both short-term planning based on projected needs and demands as well as the 100-year master plan.

Cook Children's Medical Center—South Tower (Fort Worth, Texas) A 314,000-square-foot expansion connecting to original Main Hospital building on Cook Children's campus; the new building will expand the emergency care facilities and provide additional space for a new Heart Center. In association with FKP Architects, Inc. and RTKL.

2011

Reston Mixed-Use Master Plan (Reston, Virginia) Conceptual master-planning studies for a walkable mixed-use development on a 98-acre parcel predominated by suburban-office and surface parking.

The Woodley (Washington, D.C.) Exterior design for an eight-story, 212-unit rental apartment building adjacent to the Marriot Wardman Park Hotel; interior design for common public spaces, including the lobby, lounge, club, library and study and the ground-floor corridors. In association with VOA, Cooper Carry, and Michael Vergason Landscape Architects.

2010

1275 Pennsylvania Avenue (Washington, D.C.) New metal and glass office entry marquee, improvements to the garage entry ramp, gutting and redesign of the office lobby and entrance sequence, and renovation of typical floor elevator and restrooms, plus exterior re-skin of the lower three floors. In association with Hickok Cole Architects and Davis Construction.

The Cassidy & Trust Buildings (Fort Worth, Texas) Six-story, multiuse building adjacent to the Sanger Lofts and the Fakes Building, with retail and an office lobby on the ground floor topped by four floors of office space; six penthouse residential units on the sixth floor connect to the sixth-floor circulation of the existing Sanger Lofts. In association with Bennett Benner Partners and Dunaway Associates.

The Commerce Building (Fort Worth, Texas) Five-story, 84,000-square-foot mixed-use Class-A office building with ground-level retail and restaurant fronting onto Commerce Street and Sundance Square Plaza. In association with Bennett Benner Partners and Dunaway Associates.

Downtown Crown (Gaithersburg, Maryland) Façade design for over 89,000 square feet of commercial and retail space.

Hotel Guanahani & Spa (Saint Barthélemy, French West Indies) Master plan and phased renovation of a seventy-two-room hotel in the French West Indies, including major renovations to guest rooms, a new boutique, fitness center, and improvements to the site circulation and landscaping. In association with Luis Pons Design Lab and Lotus Architects.

Sundance Square (Fort Worth, Texas) A 55,000-square-foot urban plaza bisecting Main Street, which includes architectural shading elements, multiple interactive fountains, a community stage and a 2,000-square-foot pavilion. The site features two historic buildings that have been restored and adaptively reused. In association with Bennett Benner Partners, Dunaway Associates, and Michael Vergason Landscape Architects.

The Westbrook (Fort Worth, Texas) Six-story, 84,000-square-foot, mixed-use Class-A office building with ground-level retail and restaurant fronting on to Houston Street and Sundance Square Plaza. Community stage sits below a large clock tower on the central bay. In association with Bennett Benner Partners and Dunaway Associates.

2009

Donald W. Reynolds Discovery Children's Museum (Las Vegas, Nevada) Exterior façade design for a 58,000-square-foot, purpose-built children's museum on the campus of Symphony Park, site of the Smith Center for the Performing Arts. In association with HKS Architects, Martin & Martin, Walter P. Moore, and Green Building Services.

Fort Worth Arena (Fort Worth, Texas) Design for a new 560,000-square-foot arena sited on the Will Rogers Memorial Center campus, including a 156,000-square-foot livestock support center and a 215,000-square-foot landscaped plaza. When not in use for livestock events, the bowl has been designed to accommodate hockey, family shows, NCAA regulation basketball tournaments, and concerts.

Orioles Spring Training Facilities at Ed Smith Stadium (Sarasota, Florida) Master plan and building design for the renovation and expansion of the Baltimore Orioles facilities at Ed Smith Stadium and Buck O'Neil Baseball Complex. An 85,000-square-foot, two-level concourse addition; increased existing seating from 6,500 to 9,000; and 15,000-square-foot additions and 46,000-square-foot renovations to two existing clubhouses. In association with Hoyt Architects.

Saratoga Racetrack (Saratoga Springs, New York) Phased revitalization via historic renovation, adaptive reuse, and judicious new construction of the oldest continually operating sports venue in America.

2008

13|U (13th and U Streets, Washington, D.C.) A 173,000-square-foot, 138-unit rental apartment building with ground-level retail sited along the U Street corridor adjacent to the Cardozo Metro Station. In association with BBGM, Champalimaud and Tadjer-Cohen-Edelson Associates.

Charleston Gaillard Center (Charleston, South Carolina) Renovation and expansion for 1960s-era general purpose auditorium, including full renovation of the auditorium, expansion of exhibit hall into a banquet facility and construction of an office building that will accommodate several of the City's departmental offices. In association with Earl Swensson Associates, Evans and Schmidt Architects, Akustiks, Wertimer and Associates, and Forsberg Engineering and Surveying.

Cook Children's Medical Center Medical Office Building (Fort Worth, Texas) A 210,000-square-foot medical office building to accommodate increased outpatient and laboratory services, and connect directly to the inpatient tower of the North Shelf Expansion to allow shared services and convenient communication for physicians. In association with FKP.

Cook Children's Medical Center North Garage Expansion and Helipads (Fort Worth, Texas) A 413,000-square-foot expansion increasing the capacity of the North Garage. The garage will be expanded to the west and increased from four to six levels of parking, plus two helicopter landing pads will be located above the top parking level. In association with Intertech Design.

Cook Children's Medical Center North Shelf Expansion (Fort Worth, Texas) A 223,000-square-foot expansion of the north shelf and a new patient tower, doubling the size of the Neonatal Intensive Care Unit, including a new cafeteria and kitchen, and connecting to the existing North Pavilion patient tower on all levels. In association with FKP.

Cook Children's Medical Center South Garage Expansion (Fort Worth, Texas) A 175,000-square-foot expansion of the South Garage will be accomplished by adding two more parking levels above the existing four levels. In association with Conti, Jumper & Gardner.

Coombs Stadium (Durham, North Carolina) Conceptual Design for a new 5,000 seat A.C.C. baseball park and team facilities building designed to minor league specifications.

George Dean Johnson Jr. College of Business and Economics at the University of South Carolina Upstate (Spartanburg, South Carolina) A 60,000-square-foot Business School located downtown adjacent to the Chapman Cultural Center as part of the Renaissance Park Development. In association with McMillan Smith & Partners PLLC, Britt Peters and Associates Inc., Wade Crow Consulting Engineers, and Matrix Engineering Inc.

Southlake Office and Retail Building (Southlake, Texas) A 25,000-square-foot, full-block footprint, two-story office over high-end retail with three distinct façades. In association with The Beck Group.

Urbana (Fredrick County, Maryland) Preliminary site plan studies and conceptual design for approximately 600,000 square feet of retail development on a 94-acre site.

2007

12711 Twinbrook Parkway (Twinbrook, Maryland) A 200,000-square-foot speculative office building representing the final phase build-out of an 800,000-square-foot, 16-acre office, and research and development master plan. The building's design incorporates numerous sustainable features and is targeting a LEED Gold rating.

440 First Street NW (Washington, D.C.) Renovation of an existing eight-story office building to design new skin, lobby, and additional floor. In association with Inter Spec Design, Inc., Tadjer-Cohen-Edelson Associates, Inc., and META Engineers, P.C.

Caesars Entertainment Master Plan (Las Vegas, Nevada) Long-range master plan for a casino on the Las Vegas Strip with mixed-use development to increase overall value of holdings (uses may include upgrades of existing hotels, additional hotels and residential towers, additional retail, possible exhibit/convention center).

Flower Mound Central Business District Master Plan (Flower Mound, Texas) Master plan for the development of a 158-acre site near the center of Flower Mound's primary commercial area, featuring numerous parks, squares, and a central river walk surrounded by residential, office, retail, and medical uses.

High Street (Atlanta, Georgia) Master plan for the redevelopment of a 45-acre parcel adjacent to the Dunwoody MARTA rail station, including 2,500 residential units, 300,000 square feet of retail, 200,000/350,000 square feet of hotel/office uses. In association with Kimley-Horn and Associates.

The Linq (Las Vegas, Nevada) A 390,000-square-foot retail and dining district adjacent to Caesars Palace anchored by a 550-foot-tall observation wheel. In association with Klai Juba Architects and WA Richardson Builders LLC.

Lon Evans Corrections Center (Fort Worth, Texas) A new adult detention facility located in downtown Forth Worth, the building will occupy a single city block and will connect to the county's existing jail located across the street. In association with Gideon-Toal Architects and Wiginton Hooker Jeffry Architects.

2006

Merriweather Post Pavilion Renovation (Columbia, Maryland) Site studies, planning, and renovation analysis.

Regent Square (Houston, Texas) Planning and partial design of a mixed-use urban development with 330,000 square feet of retail and restaurant uses, 1,740 residential units, 60,000 square feet of office space, and a 200-room hotel. In association with Morris Architects, Robert A.M. Stern Architects LLP, Bowie Gridley Architects, B&D Studios LLC, Aponwao Design Inc., Hartman-Cox, GRG Inc., and Haynes Whaley Associates Inc.

The Smith Center for the Performing Arts (Las Vegas, Nevada) State-of-the-art 2,055-seat multipurpose hall, a small 600-seat theater, and a cabaret theater. In association with HKS Architects, The Whiting-Turner Contracting Company, MSA Engineering Consultants, Walter P. Moore, Fisher Dachs Associates, Akustiks, LLC, and Green Building Services.

University of Miami Space Study (Coral Gables, Florida) Provisions for the addition of new buildings to the existing 265-acre Coral Gables campus over the next twenty to thirty years, through a study and remapping of the overall structure of open space, and pedestrian and vehicular circulation networks through and around campus.

2005

Carnegie Building (Fort Worth, Texas) A 280,000-square-foot, sixteen-story Class-A office building in Sundance Square. In association with Boka Powell LLC, Blum Consulting Engineers, and Datum Engineers.

Hillview Master Plan (Denton, Texas) A 440-acre, mixed-use residential and commercial development.

The Palladium at the Center for the Performing Arts (Carmel, Indiana) A 1,600-seat concert hall and 500-seat multiuse theater to anchor Carmel's new mixed-use downtown development. In association with CSO Architects, Artec Consultants, Lynch, Harrison & Brumleve, and L'Acquis Consulting Engineer.

Newport Beach Resort (Port Aransas, Texas) Development of 225,000 square feet to include residential space and golf club.

Twinbrook Office Building (Twinbrook, Maryland) Design for a 350,000-square-foot, thirteen-story office building with ground-floor retail.

2004

1800 Rockville Pike (Rockville, Maryland) Retail and residential development on a 4.5-acre site in downtown Rockville.

Chapman Cultural Center (Spartanburg, South Carolina) A space of 82,000 square feet to house eight independent organizations: Art Museum, History Museum, Music Foundation, Science Center, Arts Guild, The Arts Partnership, Ballet School, and a 500-seat theater. In association with Little Diversified Architectural Consulting, Linbeck Construction Company, Jim Metze, McCracken Clopel, and Creative Acoustics.

Le Bonheur Childrens Medical Center (Memphis, Tennessee) New construction of a 230-bed Children's Hospital. In association with FKP Architects, Inc., Walter P. Moore and Associates, Inc., Smith Seckman Reid, and Linbeck Construction Corporation.

Private Vacation Residence (High Desert Location) A 16,050-square-foot Frank Lloyd Wright–style textile home with a pool house and a garage with an apartment above. In association with Tom Rees Construction and Robert Sillman Associates.

2003

Cattle Raiser's Museum (Fort Worth, Texas) Museum located in Fort Worth's downtown Western Heritage Center and intended to link to the National Cowgirl Museum and Hall of Fame. In association with Gideon-Toal.

Duke University Central Campus Master Plan (Durham, North Carolina) Master plan for a 250-acre area between Duke's two historic campuses to be developed as a new mixed-use university village, including residential, office, retail development, and plans for a campus-wide transportation system. In association with Cousins Prep.

Firewheel Town Center (Garland, Texas) A 775,000-square-foot mixed-use complex located in Dallas–Fort Worth metroplex. In association with Beck Architecture, Zinser Grossman Structural, and ARJO Engineers.

Vanderbilt University (Nashville, Tennessee) Master plan and conceptual design for development of 1,600-bed freshman campus on Vanderbilt's historic Peabody campus and plans for the creation of 4,500 residential college housing units for the upper class-level population on the main campus.

2002

Mount Vernon Walk (Washington, D.C.) Architectural design of the large, urban development won in a design competition with eleven development teams; design includes 500 affordable and market-rate housing units, artists' live/work studios, a pedestrian promenade, 57,000 square feet of retail, and a live performance theater.

Parkway Center Master Plan (Las Vegas, Nevada) Master plan for mixed-use development of a 61-acre site adjacent to the downtown area.

Private Vacation Residence (New England) Design for the new construction of a private residence, guest house, and pool on a beachfront estate. In association with Sourati Engineering Group and Knight/Zadeh.

Schermerhorn Symphony Center (Nashville, Tennessee) Design of a new 1,900-seat concert hall for the Nashville Symphony Orchestra. In association with Earl Swenson Associates and Hastings Architecture Associates, KSI Engineers, I.C. Thomasson & Associates, Akustiks Inc., and American Constructors.

2001

Arabian Horse Heritage Center (Fort Worth, Texas) Planning and site design for a new museum.

Dr Pepper Ballpark (Frisco, Texas) A 10,000-seat, twenty-four-suite, minor league ballpark for the Class AA affiliate of the Texas Rangers, serving as the focal point for the 70-acre, Stars City development. In association with HKS Architects, Centex Construction Company, and G.W. Vines.

Mount Vernon Walk (Washington, D.C.) Architectural concept design for 400 housing units and 40,000 square feet of community retail for a development rights competition for a 3.2-acre in-town site.

Stars City Master Plan (Frisco, Texas) Master planning and site design for a new, mixed-use development including a hotel, conference center, ice rink, and a minor league ballpark.

2000

Cook Children's Medical Center, Hospital Inpatient Expansion—North Pavilion (Fort Worth, Texas) A new 150,000-square-foot addition to the hospital that contains rehab and neonatal units, patient room floors, offices, classrooms, and an auditorium. In association with FKP Architects, Inc. and Linbeck Construction Company.

Cook Children's Medical Center, Outpatient Surgery Expansion (Fort Worth, Texas) Design of additional emergency services and building expansion as part of the hospital's master plan. In association with FKP Architects, Inc.

Frisco Phase I Buildings (Frisco, Texas) Design for mixed-use buildings that include both apartments and office spaces over retail spaces.

Frisco Square (Frisco, Texas) The master plan for the 140-acre site calls for a mixed-use development and strives to emphasize pedestrian use through the inclusion of arcades and shared green spaces. In association with Parker Croston.

Grand Avenue (Southlake, Texas) Design for part of a retail and office building in the Southlake Town Square master plan as designed by David M. Schwarz Architects. In association with Bowie Gridley, Urban Architecture, Beck Group, Bury & Partners- FW Inc., and L.A. Fuess Partners.

Hawken School Master Plan (Cleveland, Ohio) Master planning and programming for a private middle and upper school on two campuses, including landscaping, building design, and location for the new and existing facilities.

Hawken School Natatorium (Cleveland, Ohio) Design for a 27,00-square-foot pool building that includes a new, shared lobby with existing athletic facilities, and a competitive swimming and diving pool. In association with Collins Gordon Bostwick Architects.

New York City Apartment (New York, New York) Interior design and furnishings for a 3,600-square-foot apartment on Central Park West.

North Shore Housing and Garage (Pittsburgh, Pennsylvania) Design for a new residential building and garage in the North Shore area of Pittsburgh.

Parker Square (Flower Mound, Texas) Design of two additional retail/office buildings that are part of a 24-acre town square master plan. In association with Vidaud + Associates for Buildings 900 and 800; also in association with FM Parker Square, Ltd.

Private Residence (Fort Worth, Texas) Renovation and minor addition to an historic home for a small family.

Rhine House Restoration (St. Helena, California) Restoration of the historic Rhine House Mansion on the Beringer Vineyards, using new wood casework that will delineate smaller spaces within the original winery and will complement the palette of the original stone structure. In association with Architectural Resources Group.

Texas Rangers Master Plan Update (Arlington, Texas) Revision and expansion of the scope of the original master plan to increase pedestrian-oriented, mixed-use development adjacent to all sides of the existing major league ballpark.

1999

Bank One Building (Fort Worth, Texas) Design for a twelve-story, 285,000-square-foot office building with an attached nine-story garage in an urban setting offering retail space on the ground level, and loft-style office space on the other eleven floors; the building creates a link between the rich architectural past of Fort Worth and its high-tech business environment of today. In association with HKS Architects, Linbeck Construction Company, Datum Engineering, and James Johnston & Associates.

Cook Children's Medical Center, Ancillary Services Building (Fort Worth, Texas) A new 125,000-square-foot building to house information systems, administration, and office space.

Cook Children's Medical Center, North Garage (Fort Worth, Texas) Design for a new 600-car garage as part of the hospital's master plan.

Florida Marlins Ballpark (South Florida) Site selection, planning, and design of a major league ballpark for the Florida Marlins Baseball Club, the design envisions lushly landscaped tropical concourses and a unique retractable roof that maximizes fan comfort.

Pittsburgh Planning (Pittsburgh, Pennsylvania) Master planning for revitalizing a waterfront warehouse district, including new and converted buildings and a realigned street grid to reconnect the area with downtown.

The Presidio of California (San Francisco, California) Design Advisors to the Presidio Trust for the conversion of the 1,480-acre, former military base to an urban national park.

Southlake Town Hall (Southlake, Texas) A new 80,000-square-foot City Hall, housing both city and county functions along with a courtroom, city council chambers, and a new public library. In association with GSI Architects and BL&P Engineers, Inc.

Tarrant County Family Law Center (Fort Worth, Texas) Design for a 375,000-square-foot county court building that includes twenty-eight Family and Civil District court rooms. In association with Gideon/Toal. Inc., The Facility Group, Inc., Davidson Design Group, Inc., Summit Consultants, Inc., R.L. Woods & Associates, and Gilbane.

Victory Plaza (Dallas, Texas) Master planning and design of a 2-acre urban plaza in Victory, an urban development in downtown Dallas. As a forecourt to the American Airlines Center that includes two five-story, mixed-use, retail/office buildings that surround the plaza. In association with HKS Inc.

1998

280 Forest Drive (North Haven, New York) Design of a 5,500-square-foot private residence on a waterfront bluff. In association with William J. Reese, Architect.

American Airlines Center (Dallas, Texas) Design of a 750,000-square-foot arena, a new home for the Dallas Mavericks and Dallas Stars, with seating for 18,500; will be the centerpiece of a 60-acre urban development adjacent to downtown Dallas. In association with HKS Architects, Austin Commercial Contractors, Walter P Moore & Associates, and Flack + Kurtz.

Chateau St. Jean (Sonoma Valley, California) A 5,000-square-foot new hospitality center with a 1.5-acre formal courtyard at an historic winery. In association with Hall and Bartley Architects and Paragon General Contractors.

Cityplace Master Plan (Dallas, Texas) Conceptual design for a master plan for a 31-acre track in Dallas for mixed-use office, retail, and hotel development. In association with HKS Architects, Austin Commercial, Brockett, Davis, Brock, Inc., and James Johnston & Associates.

Cityplace Office and Retail Building (Dallas, Texas) Design for the first office building to be developed under the Cityplace Master Plan, an eight-story main building, two retail buildings, and 700-car garage. In association with HKS Architects.

Cityplace Village (Dallas, Texas) Conceptual design of a mixed-use residential and retail development.

Guesthouse in Rocky Mountains (Snowmass Village, Colorado) Design and interiors for a new 4,200-square-foot log guesthouse.

Miami Intermodal Center (Miami, Florida) A mixed-use, waterfront development complex encompassing retail, office, hotel, residential, entertainment, and parking.

Private Residence (Aspen, Colorado) Renovation of a nineteenth-century dairy barn into a vacation home.

Stonebriar (Dallas, Texas) Conceptual master plan for a large mixed-used retail and office development north of Dallas.

West Village (Dallas, Texas) Mixed-use retail and residential development with 150,000 square feet of retail space, 200 condominium apartments and a 700-car garage. In association with KSNG Architect and Basharkah Engineering, Inc.

1997

Beringer Vineyards Master Plan (St. Helena, California) Master plan for an existing 17-acre vineyard, including renovation of visitor center, office, the old distillery, and outbuildings.

Southlake Town Square (Southlake, Texas) Design for a two-block square surrounded by retail shops, offices, restaurants, and a new City Hall. In association with Urban Architecture for Phase I.

Stag's Leap Vineyards Master Plan (Napa Valley, California) Master plan for the improvement of a 38-acre vineyard and its outbuildings. In association with Architectural Resources Group and Paragon General Contractors.

1996

60 Auberge Road (Napa Valley, California) Renovation/addition to a 1950 vineyard house. In association with More Associates.

2710 Chain Bridge Road (Washington, D.C.) Library, kitchen, and master bedroom addition to a previously expanded Victorian-style cottage.

3465 Macomb Street Addition (Washington, D.C.) Renovation/addition to a private residence.

Dallas Arts District Master Plan (Dallas, Texas) Master plan for three blocks in the Dallas Arts District; a mixed-use development, including residential, commercial, and entertainment facilities.

Cook Children's Medical Center, Medical Office Building (Fort Worth, Texas) Four-story, 83,500-square-foot office building on the CMC Campus. In association with FKP Architects, Inc.

Cook Children's Medical Center, South Extension (Fort Worth, Texas) Addition to main hospital block of Medical Center Campus, to include expansion of the cafeteria, conference facilities and bridge connection to parking garage and medical office building. In association with FKP Architects, Inc.

Flower Mound Town Master Plan (Flower Mound, Texas) A 24-acre retail and office development organized along two main streets that front a traditional town green.

Fort Worth Public Library, First Floor Interior (Fort Worth, Texas) Over 50,000 square feet of finished interiors, which includes grand lobby spaces, a children's and media library. In association with Hidell Architects.

Maddox Muse Rehearsal/Concert Hall Facility (Fort Worth, Texas) The 70,000-square-foot support complex for Bass Hall, including rehearsal halls, studios, and arts organizations office spaces. In association with HKS Architects.

Severance Hall (Cleveland, Ohio) Restoration, renovation and 40,000-square-foot expansion of the landmark Severance Hall, home of the Cleveland Orchestra. In association with GSI Architects.

Sid Richardson Museum of Western Art (Fort Worth, Texas) Renovation of an existing public gallery and nonprofit offices, including code upgrades and a new entry façade (includes the National Gallery of Art).

Southlake Master Plan (Southlake, Texas) Twenty-year master plan for a new downtown based on a traditional town grid; 2.7 million square feet of commercial development accommodated on the 130-acre site.

Texas Pacific Group Offices (Washington, D.C.) Design, furnishing and finishes for a 4,000-square-foot office suite. In association with A.I. Boggs.

Western Heritage Center (Fort Worth, Texas) Site selection and master plan for cultural complex, including three museums.

Worthington Hotel Ballroom, Conference Center (Fort Worth, Texas) Final phase of a three-phase project; the 74,000-square-foot renovation of main and secondary ballrooms, meeting rooms, and lobby spaces to convey a regional flair. In association with Vidaud + Associates.

1995

Barnes & Noble Bookstore (Fort Worth, Texas) Interior design for a two-story, 28,000-square-foot downtown bookstore and café. In association with Antunovich Associates.

Chicago Bears Stadium (Chicago, Illinois) Architectural consultation to the Chicago Bears in their efforts to build a new 75,000-seat football stadium.

Cook Children's Medical Center, Central Plant (Fort Worth, Texas) Central heating and cooling plant for the Medical Center Campus. In association with FKP Architects Inc.

Lake Las Vegas (Henderson, Nevada) Development assessment and preliminary master planning for a 2,200-acre mixed-use development around a 320-acre artificial lake.

National Cowgirl Museum and Hall of Fame (Fort Worth, Texas) The 40,000-square-foot new hall of fame and museum in the Fort Worth Cultural District. In association with Gideon/Toal.

Private Lodge (Snowmass Village, Colorado) Owner consultation and interior architecture and design for a 16,000-square-foot new construction: a log residence and caretaker's cottage, including selection, purchasing and placement of furnishings and artworks.

Worthington Hotel Lobby and Restaurant (Fort Worth, Texas) Phase II of a three-phase project, the renovation of the main lobby and a Star of Texas Grill and Restaurant. In association with Huitt/Zollars.

Yale University Environmental Science Center (New Haven, Connecticut) A 96,000-square-foot laboratory, teaching and storage facility for the Yale Institute for Biospheric Studies, a new interdisciplinary environmental science center; an addition to the Peabody Museum. In association with GSI Architects.

1994

Blockbuster Park Master Plan Team (South Florida) Venue architects for arena and stadium components of a 3,000-acre sports and entertainment complex in Dade and Broward Counties, Florida.

Dinnerware Design Design of five patterns of porcelain china for Architectural Objects, Inc.

Disney's Wide World of Sports Complex (Orlando, Florida) Design of a 6,500-seat field house and a 7,500-seat baseball park in a complex of varied sports venues. In association with HKS Architects.

Preview Center at the BoardWalk (Orlando, Florida) New construction of a 26,000-square-foot clubhouse that will function as the central marketing facility for the Disney Vacation Club.

Wells Fargo Building (Fort Worth, Texas) Design of a five-story downtown office building with bank, restaurant, and retail space at street level. In association with HKS Architects.

1993

Corporate Headquarters Master Plan (Fort Worth, Texas) Master plan for 1.9-million-square-foot corporate headquarters campus on eleven city blocks with seven separate buildings, a 280 foot long span network control facility, and garage space for 3,000 cars.

Montessori School (Fort Worth, Texas) New façade in De Stijl style for an existing building.

Nancy Lee and Perry R. Bass Performance Hall (Fort Worth, Texas) A 2,100-seat performing arts hall to house the Fort Worth Ballet, the Fort Worth Opera, the Fort Worth Symphony Orchestra, and the quadrennial Van Cliburn International Piano Competition. In association with HKS Architects.

New York Botanical Gardens Library/ Herbarium (New York, New York) New building to contain a 5.5-million-specimen herbarium and botanical library, and renovation of portions of the landmark Museum Building for the public areas of the library.

Sundance East (Fort Worth, Texas) Ten-theater multiplex cinema and 55,000 square feet of retail and commercial office space occupying a full downtown block. In association with HKS Architects.

1992

Cook-Fort Worth Children's Medical Center (Fort Worth, Texas) Master plan and 120,000-square-foot addition, including expansion of the cafeteria and conference facilities.

Fort Worth Public Library (Fort Worth, Texas) A 200,000-square-foot expansion and master plan for the central library. In association with Growald Architects.

Mount Zion (Front Royal, Virginia) Renovation and master plan of a 4,500-square-foot historic residence and 300+-acre site.

New York Botanical Gardens Master Plan (New York, New York) Master planning for the further growth of the Botanical Gardens campus to accommodate a new library/herbarium, restaurant, catering facility, and visitors center.

Oak Grove (Marshall, Virginia) Addition to existing four-bedroom country house, including new swimming pool and landscaping.

Shanghai/Cypress (Shanghai, Peoples Republic of China) Master plan and design of buildings on a 50-acre site, including a 120-room hotel, 240 apartment units, a restaurant in a restored historic building, an athletic club, and eighty luxury villas.

Whydah Pirates Complex (Charlestown Navy Yard. Boston, Massachusetts) A 150,000-square-foot entertainment/educational facility dedicated to the history of pirates.

Worthington Hotel (Fort Worth, Texas) Renovation and upgrade of 506-room hotel to Five Star level with new furnishings and finishes to convey a regional flavor. In association with Yandell and Hiller.

1991

Rock Hill Farm (Front Royal, Virginia) Renovation of a 5,500-square-foot residence on a 700+-acre site.

Texas Rangers Ballpark (Arlington, Texas) Design for a 48,000-seat stadium complex awarded as result of nationwide design competition. Completed in association with HKS Architects.

Texas Rangers Ballpark Master Plan (Arlington, Texas) Master plan for the 300-acre site surrounding the new Texas Rangers Ballpark.

1990

2601 31st Street NW (Washington, D.C.) Subsequent phase renovation of 1985 project, including 2,000-square-foot addition and numerous interior alterations.

2853 Ontario Road NW (Washington, D.C.) A 2,900-square-foot apartment renovation.

I-395 Air Rights Project (Washington, D.C.) A 1.9-million-square-foot office space, 250,000-square-foot hotel, 250,000-square-foot apartment building, mixed-use project originally submitted for the F.C.C. headquarters, revised for presentation to the G.S.A. for the E.P.A.

Pentagon Square (Arlington County, Virginia) A 1.1 million-square-foot speculative office space plus rezoning studies to include 50,000 to 80,000 square feet of retail and up to 120 apartments. Presented to G.S.A. and D.O.D.

Penthouse Apartment (Fort Worth, Texas) Custom, 3,500-square-foot residence on two floors plus loft in Sundance West Apartment Building.

Sanger Lofts (Fort Worth, Texas) Conversion of 75,000-square-foot department store to loft apartments. In association with Terry M. Harden Architects for construction phase observations.

Sundance 11 AMC Cinemas (Fort Worth, Texas) Interior design of an eleven-screen multiplex cinema. In association with HDR.

Sundance Master Plan (Fort Worth, Texas) Urban center master plan for Fort Worth.

1989

500 Park Avenue Penthouse (New York, New York) A 8,500-square-foot two-story apartment.

1217 Potomac Street NW (Washington, D.C.) Renovation/ addition of 4,000-square-foot historic residence into gallery/office for a private art collector.

2215 30th Street NW (Washington, D.C.) "Art Gallery" addition to a 20,000-square-foot private residence.

Design for a Wedding (Washington, D.C.) Design for a wedding ceremony and reception space for 240 guests.

Jefferson Place/M Street NW (Square 139, Washington, D.C.) A 400,000-square-foot office building and retail space in the central business district, incorporating existing historic row houses.

Mount Vernon Square East (Square 515, Washington, D.C.) Mixed-use project of 290 apartments, 52,000-square-foot commercial and retail space, and a 6,500-square-foot community building.

Natelli Woods Lane (Avenell, Maryland) New single-family residence of 17,300 square feet.

Square 185 (16th and I Streets NW, Washington, D.C.) A 308,000-square-foot office building with views to the White House.

Square 515 (Washington, D.C.) Mixed-use project of 290 apartments, 52,000 square feet of commercial and retail, and a 6,500-square-foot community building.

1988

1201 F Street NW (Washington, D.C.) Twelve story, 238,000-square-foot new office/retail building, with 69,000 square feet of underground parking. In association with Irrera Studio Arts.

1437 Rhode Island Avenue NW (Washington, D.C.) A 400-unit new apartment building.

Hollywood Plaza (Hollywood, California) Urban mixed-use project of 1.4 million square feet, including 1,000 apartments, office and retail space, and a health club.

Square 456/Hecht Company Building (Washington, D.C.) New construction, 240,000 square feet office/retail component of a 2-million-square-foot complex, retaining historic façades in the Downtown Historic District.

1987

14th & F Streets NW (Washington, D.C.) Design for new construction, 162,000-square-foot office/retail for the Westory Building, incorporating an existing 22,000-square-foot historic structure.

17 Primrose Street (Chevy Chase, Maryland) Renovation of a 5,000-square-foot private residence.

500 Park Avenue (New York, New York) Renovation of a 1,800-square-foot apartment.

1050 15th Street NW (Washington, D.C.) Lobby redesign for a commercial office building.

1133 Connecticut Avenue NW (Washington, D.C.) New construction of a 227,000-square-foot office/retail building. In association with Vlastimil Koubek, Fairmont Builders.

1301 L Street NW (Washington, D.C.) A 286,000-square-foot, twelve-story new Planned Unit Development office building, with 90,000 square feet of underground parking.

1312 Massachusetts Avenue NW (Washington, D.C.) A 200,000-square-foot, 134-unit new construction of Planned Unit Development apartment building.

2840 Woodland Drive NW (Washington, D.C.) Renovation/addition to an 8,300-square-foot private residence, originally designed by Clarke Waggaman in 1917.

3106 N Street NW (Washington, D.C.) Façade and garden redesign for a private residence.

4511 28th Street NW (Washington, D.C.) Renovation of a 5,200-square-foot private residence.

The Forum at Park Lane (Dallas, Texas) New construction, 310,000-square-foot retirement community. In association with Parker Croston.

Mount Vernon East (Washington, D.C.) Master plan for a 1.6-million-square-foot phased commercial/residential development.

Square 247 (Washington, D.C.) New 321,000-square-foot office building and conversion of an existing 85,000-square-foot office building to residential, as Planned Unit Development.

Sundance West (Fort Worth, Texas) Twelve-story, 250,000-square-foot multiuse office, retail, cinema, condominium building. In association with HDR.

1986

316 Houston Street (Fort Worth, Texas) Renovation of a 5,000-square-foot office.

415 Prince Street (Alexandria, Virginia) Renovation of a 9,000-square-foot "Governor's House" (1802–10) for a private residence.

500 N. Water Street (Milwaukee, Wisconsin) Renovation of historic seven-story warehouse for office use.

555 Eleventh Street/The Lincoln Building (Washington, D.C.) A 480,000-square-foot new office/retail building, incorporating existing façades and located in the Pennsylvania Avenue National Historic Site. In association with Swanke, Hayden, Connell.

819 N. Marshall Street (Milwaukee, Wisconsin) Renovation/addition of an 80,000-square-foot historic duplex for office use.

900 15th Street NW (Washington, D.C.) Façade redesign for the United Mine Workers Building.

1451 N. Prospect Street (Milwaukee, Wisconsin) Renovation of a 25,000-square-foot historic church for office/retail use.

2030 24th Street NW (Washington, D.C.) Renovation/addition to a private residence designed by Paul Cret in 1938.

2039 New Hampshire Avenue NW (Washington, D.C.) Renovation of a condominium in an historic apartment building.

2133 Wisconsin Avenue NW (Washington, D.C.) Feasibility study for the renovation of four buildings into a single office/retail mixed-use complex.

2213 M Street NW (Washington, D.C.) "City Cafe," a 2,740-square-foot, 100-seat restaurant/bar interior.

2424 California Street NW (Washington, D.C.) Renovation of a 9,000-square-foot villa (circa 1900).

2960 Georgia Avenue NW (Washington, D.C.) Feasibility study for a 250,000-square-foot mixed-use office, retail, and residential Planned Unit Development.

3465 Macomb Street NW (Washington, D.C.) Renovation/ addition to a 5,400-square-foot private residence.

5032 Lowell Street NW (Washington, D.C.) Renovation/addition to a private residence.

6832 Wilson Lane (Bethesda, Maryland) Phase II renovation/addition to a private residence.

Law Offices (Washington, D.C.) Design for law offices.

Pennsylvannia Avenue Development Corporation Lansburgh's Competition (E Street NW, Washington, D.C.) A 683,000-square-foot construction/ renovation of a mixed-use development, including office space, apartments, retail, movie theaters, health club, and the Corcoran School of Art.

The Saratoga (4601 Connecticut Avenue NW, Washington, D.C.) A 186-unit, ten-story new Planned Unit Development apartment building.

Square 166 (Washington, D.C.) New 179,000-square-foot office/retail building.

Square 698/1100 South Capitol Street (Washington, D.C.) A 146,000-square-foot new office building for a Planned Unit Development.

1985

650 Pennsylvania Avenue NW (Washington, D.C.) Design for a 2,000-square-foot walk-in medical treatment center.

955 26th Street NW (Washington, D.C.) Design for a 2,300-square-foot custom apartment.

2601 31st Street NW (Washington, D.C.) Renovation of a 6,800-square-foot private residence.

4922-A Saint Elmo Avenue (Bethesda, Maryland) Redesign for an office building entry.

Cook-Fort Worth Children's Medical Center (Fort Worth, Texas) New construction of a 265,000-square-foot 169-bed children's hospital. In association with Karlsberger Architects.

Westover Square (Fort Worth, Texas) Design for new construction of three 2,800-square-foot attached speculative residences.

1984

64 Ocean Drive (North Shores, Delaware) Design for a new 5,000-square-foot beach house.

410 West 7th Street (Fort Worth, Texas) Renovation of an office building lobby.

512 9th Street NW (Washington, D.C.) Renovation of an office building lobby.

700 Chain Bridge Road (McLean, Virginia) Renovation/addition to a 31,000-square-foot "Merrywood" estate.

955 26th Street NW (Washington, D.C.) Design for a 4,500-square-foot, ninth-floor penthouse apartment.

955 26th Street NW (Washington, D.C.) Design for a 4,400-square-foot, eighth-floor apartment.

2871 Tilden Street NW (Washington, D.C.) Renovation/addition to a private residence.

Autobahn Imports (Fort Worth, Texas) Renovation of Volvo/Porsche/Audi dealership showroom.

Central Park Master Plan (Dallas, Texas) Land planning and architecture for a 42-acre, 3.6-million-square-foot mixed-use development, including office buildings, a retirement community, and a church.

Cooksey Drive/"Rosecliff" (Seal Harbor, Maine) Renovation of a 10,000-square-foot vacation estate.

"Downtown Stages" Theater (Washington, D.C.) Study of incentives for development of legitimate theater in Downtown Washington, D.C., through the Washington League of Theatres.

Irving Shops (Irving, Texas) Redesign of a 228,000-square-foot shopping center.

Potomac Avenue NW (Washington, D.C.) Two speculative houses of approximately 2,500 square feet each.

River Hills (Fort Worth, Texas) Land planning and architecture for 1,200-acre development.

The Ulysses S. Grant House (3238 R Street NW, Washington, D.C.) Renovation of an historic estate for a private residence.

1983

433 Rivercrest Drive (Fort Worth, Texas) Renovation of a single-family residence.

801 Pennsylvania Avenue SE (Washington, D.C.) Renovation of a 50,000-square-foot historic Capitol Hill building for office use.

1072-74 Thomas Jefferson Street NW (Washington, D.C.) Renovation/restoration mixed-use project in the Georgetown Historic District.

1600 U Street NW (Washington, D.C.) Renovation/addition to 14,000-square-foot commercial historic structures in the Dupont Circle Historic District.

2319 Bancroft Place NW (Washington, D.C.) Addition to a private residence.

2710 Chain Bridge Road NW (Washington, D.C.) Renovation/addition to a 4,000-square-foot private residence.

Greensboro Plaza (Fairfax, Virginia) Schematic design for a 400,000-square-foot commercial office development.

Tysons Dulles Plaza (Fairfax, Virginia) New construction of a 700,000-square-foot mixed-use development.

Westover Square (Fort Worth, Texas) Master planning and site planning for a single-family housing development.

1982

650 Pennsylvania Avenue (Washington, D.C.) Penn Medical Building/Penmark Condominiums. A 130,000-square-foot, mixed-use development with office/retail/condominiums incorporating the art-deco façade of the Penn Theater.

2007-9 Massachusetts Avenue NW (Washington, D.C.) Renovation/conversion of the 17,000-square-foot Alice Roosevelt Longworth mansions into office use.

2350 Foxhall Road NW (Washington, D.C.) New construction of a 18,000-square-foot private residence.

3120 N Street NW (Washington, D.C.) Renovation/addition to a 10,000-square-foot private residence.

3252 R Street NW (Washington, D.C.) Attic remodeling for a private residence.

The Griffin (955 26th Street NW, Washington, D.C.) New construction of a 134,000-square-foot, nine-story condominium apartment building.

1981

1200 East Capitol Street NE (Washington, D.C.) Renovation of a sixteen-unit apartment building to condominiums.

1323 L Street NW (Washington, D.C.) New construction of an 97,000-square-foot office building with a five-story atrium.

1409 31st Street NW (Washington, D.C.) Renovation/addition to a private residence.

1729-31 Connecticut Avenue NW (Washington, D.C.) Renovation/addition to two historic 16,000-square-foot townhouses for use as office space.

1818 N Street NW (Washington, D.C.) A 130,000-square-foot new office building incorporating five existing townhouse façades.

2100 F Street NW (Washington, D.C.) Ten-story, sixty-five-unit condominium building.

2110 F Street NW (Washington, D.C.) A 70,000-square-foot, seven-story medical clinic.

2011 N Street NW (Washington, D.C.) Townhouse renovation/addition to a private residence.

3222 Scott Place NW (Washington, D.C.) Renovation of a private residence.

Main Post Office Building (Washington, D.C.) Preliminary studies for renovation of the 725,000-square-foot Washington, D.C., Main Post Office Building into offices.

1980

406 7th Street NW (Washington, D.C.) Renovation of a commercial building for major Washington art galleries.

444 K Street NW (Washington, D.C.) Preliminary study for a 286-unit apartment complex with 137,000 square feet of commercial space.

627 E Street NW (Washington, D.C.) Renovation of a commercial building.

1691 Q Street NW (Washington, D.C.) Preliminary study for 19,600-square-foot new construction loft-space condominiums.

2126 Decatur Place NW (Washington, D.C.) Renovation of a private residence.

2213 M Street NW (Washington, D.C.) New 6,000-square-foot commercial townhouse.

6832 Wilson Lane (Bethesda, Maryland) Phase I renovation/addition to a private residence.

1979

625 E Street NW (Washington, D.C.) Restaurant.

1310 Rhode Island Avenue NW (Washington, D.C.) Renovation of a townhouse for a private residence.

1312 9th Street NW (Washington, D.C.) Renovation of a townhouse into office space.

1340 Vermont Avenue NW (Washington, D.C.) Conversion/renovation of a seven-unit condominium.

1422 Euclid Street NW (Washington, D.C.) Renovation of a townhouse for a private residence.

1656 Irving Street NW (Washington, D.C.) Renovation of a townhouse for a private residence.

1700 Connecticut Avenue NW (Washington, D.C.) Renovation of a 17,000-square-foot commercial building.

1718 Connecticut Avenue NW (Washington, D.C.) New construction of a 35,000-square-foot commercial office/retail building.

1726 Euclid Street NW (Washington, D.C.) Renovation of a townhouse for a private residence.

1735 Johnson Avenue NW (Washington, D.C.) New construction of a twelve-unit condominium.

1737-41 Johnson Avenue NW (Washington, D.C.) Renovation of a warehouse into forty-six condominiums.

Foster Offices (Washington, D.C.) Design for law offices for an attorney.

Hanover Arts Project (Unit Block of N Street NW, Washington, D.C.) Planned Unit Development of a 58,000-square-foot site.

Interstate Building (418 10th Street NW, Washington, D.C.) Conversion of a 49,000-square-foot warehouse to office space.

Private Residence (Beallsville, Maryland) Design for a private residence.

1978

408 M Street NW (Washington, D.C.) Renovation of a three-unit, owner-occupied townhouse.

626 E Street NW (Washington, D.C.) Renovation of a twelve-unit apartment building.

903 M Street NW (Washington, D.C.) Renovation of a townhouse for a private residence.

1219 East Capitol Street NE (Washington, D.C.) Renovation of a townhouse for a private residence.

1341 East Capitol Street SE (Washington, D.C.) Schematic design for a twenty-four-unit apartment building.

1436 R Street NW (Washington, D.C.) Consulting architects for a twenty-eight-unit condominium.

1809 Riggs Place NW (Washington, D.C.) Renovation of a three-unit apartment building.

1810-12 Ingleside Terrace NW (Washington, D.C.) Renovation of a ten-unit condominium.

1460 Q Street NW (Washington, D.C.) New construction of a condominium apartment building.

1615 Kenyon Street NW (Washington, D.C.) Design consultants for renovation of a forty-eight-unit apartment building.

1722-24 Connecticut Avenue NW (Washington, D.C.) Commercial redevelopment of an historic townhouse in the Dupont Circle Historic District.

1734 V Street NW (Washington, D.C.) Renovation of a townhouse for a private residence.

7713 Elba Avenue (Alexandria, Virginia) Renovation/addition to a Charles Goodman–designed house.

Racquetball Club (State College, Pennsylvania) Design for a racquetball club.

1977

201 3rd Street NW (Washington, D.C.) Renovation of a townhouse for a private residence.

203 3rd Street NW (Washington, D.C.) Renovation of a townhouse for a private residence.

1444 Corcoran Street NW (Washington, D.C.) Renovation of a five-unit apartment building.

Law Offices (Washington, D.C.) Design for law offices.

Private Residence (Washington, D.C.) Landscape architecture for private residence.

Private Residence (Washington, D.C.) Renovation of a townhouse.

Private Residence (Washington, D.C.) Roof deck landscape architecture.

Private Residence (Washington, D.C.) Renovation of a townhouse.

Transition Offices (Washington, D.C.) Design for the transition offices for a national politician.

1976

Flying Cloud Inn (New Marlboro, Massachusetts) Conversion of a barn into a guest house and meeting rooms.

Private Residence (Palm Springs, California) Design of a private residence.

Private Residence (Harper's Ferry, West Virginia) Conversion of a summer cottage into a private residence.

Shapell Homes (Los Angeles, California) Redesign of existing house plans for Shapell Industries.

1975

Offices (White Plains, New York) Executive offices for Health Group.

Private Residence (Sparkill, New York) Renovation of a Victorian country house.

1973

Private Residence (Tenafly, New Jersey) Renovation/addition to a private residence.

Private Residence (Tenafly, New Jersey) Addition to a private residence.

Private Residence (New York, New York) Design of a children's environment for a private residence.

Private Residence (Santa Cruz, Patsulik, Guatamala) Design of a vacation house.

Solar House Film (New York, New York) Footage on solar house for World Energy Conference film for Film Counselors.

1972

Private Residence (Bel Air, California) Design of a private residence.

Private Residence (Red Way, California) Design of owner-built home for a private residence.

Shapell Housing (Los Angeles, California) Study of prototypical housing for Shapell Industries.

1971

Private Residence (Cape Haze, Florida) Design of a private residence.

Private Residence (Stowe, Vermont) Design of a vacation house.

SELECT AWARDS

David M. Schwarz

2015 The Richard H. Driehaus Prize (Body of Work)

2014 ICA&A Arthur Ross Award (Body of Work)

13|U (13th and U Streets, Washington, D.C.)

2018 Society of American Registered Architects Design Award of Excellence

2017 Architectural Precast Association Award for Excellence

1133 Connecticut Avenue NW (Washington, D.C.)

1991 Society of American Registered Architects (SARA), Professional Design Awards Program

1988 The Masonry Institute, Special Achievement Design Award

1718 Connecticut Avenue NW (Washington, D.C.)

2016 DC Preservation League 45th Anniversary Award

1984 The Masonry Institute, Design Award

1818 N Street NW (Washington, D.C.)

1985 The Masonry Institute, Design Award

Alpharetta City Hall (Alpharetta, Georgia)

2016 National Terrazzo and Mosaic Association Honor Award

American Airlines Center (Dallas, Texas)

2007 *Dallas Observer*, Readers Pick, Best Sports Venue

2006 *Pollstar Magazine*, Concert Venue of the Year

2003 Society of American Registered Architects, Design Award of Merit

2003 Society of American Registered Architects (California Council), Design Award for Excellence

2003 *Dallas Observer*, Best Sports Venue

2002 *Dallas Observer*, Best Sports Venue

2002 *Athletic Business Magazine*, Twenty-Second Annual Facilities of Merit, Facility of Merit Award

2002 American Council of Engineering Companies, Honor Award—Structural Engineering, Walter P. Moore, Best Engineering Project in the Nation for 2001

2002 American Council of Engineering Companies, Highest Honor—The Eminent Conceptor Award, Walter P. Moore, Most Outstanding Project in the Nation for 2001

2002 Association of General Contractors of Texas, Summit Award, 2001 Outstanding Project over $30 Million

2002 *Texas Construction Magazine*, Best of 2001 Judges Award

2002 Subcontractors Association of North Texas, 2001 Outstanding Project over $25 Million and Outstanding Project Team

2002 United Masonry Contractors Association, Golden Trowel Award, Outstanding Architectural Design, Brick Winner

2001 F.W. Dodge, Best of 2001 Judges Award

2001 United States Environmental Protection Agency (EPA), Phoenix Award

2001 *Pollstar Magazine*, Best New Major Concert Venue

2001 National Terrazo & Mosaic Association, Honor Award

2001 Minority Business Development Agency, Outstanding Corporate Award for its M/WBE Achievements

2000 Minority Business Development Agency, Outstanding Corporate Award for its M/WBE Achievements

Bank One Building (Fort Worth, Texas)

2002 Society of American Registered Architects, Design Award of Honorable Mention

Carnegie Building (Fort Worth, Texas)

2009 United Masonry Contractors Association, Golden Trowel Award

Chapman Cultural Center (Spartanburg, South Carolina)

2008 Society of American Registered Architects, Professional Design Award

Charleston Gaillard Center (Charleston, South Carolina)

2021 57th Annual Making Cities Livable Merit Award

2018 Society of American Registered Architects Design Award of Honor

2017 Institute of Classical Arts and Architecture Southeast Chapter Philip Trammell Shutze Award—Commercial/Civic/Institutional

2015 City of Charleston Award for Design Excellence

The Commerce Building (Fort Worth, Texas)

2014 United Masonry Contractors Associates, Golden Trowel Award—Commercial/Industrial

Cook Children's Medical Center (Fort Worth, Texas)

2019 Precast/Prestressed Concrete Institute Design Award—Healthcare/Medical Building

1992 Building Owners and Managers Association, In Pursuit of Excellence: Building of the Year Award

1991 Society of American Registered Architects (SARA), Professional Design Awards Program

1990 Associated General Contractors of America (Fort Worth Chapter), Outstanding Building Projects Award

Design for a Wedding (Washington, D.C.)

1990 *Interiors Magazine*, Washington Design Celebration, Competition—Design Award

Dickies Arena (Fort Worth, Texas)

2021 The Innovative Design in Engineering and Architecture with Structural Steel (IDEAS^2) Awards—Projects Greater than $200 Million

2020 Palladio Awards—New Design and Construction, More than 30,000 Square Feet

2020 Precast/Prestressed Concrete Institute Design Award—Façade Only Parking Structure

Disney's Wide World of Sports Complex (Orlando, Florida)

1999 *Texas Architect Magazine*, American Institute of Architects (Fort Worth Chapter), Award of Merit

Downtown Crown (Gaithersburg, Maryland)

2017 Montgomery County Planning Board Design Excellence Award

"Downtown Stages" Theater (Washington, D.C.)

1986 Mayor's Architectural Design Awards

Dr Pepper Ballpark (Frisco, Texas)

2009 Baseball America, 5th Best Ballpark in Minor League Baseball

2009 Baseball America, 2nd Best Ballpark in Double-A Minor League Clubs

2005 Texas Topping Out 2005, Top 10 Award

2004 American Society of Landscape Architects (Texas Chapter), Honor Award

2003 BallParks.com, Best New Ballpark for 2003

2003 American Institute of Architects (Fort Worth Chapter), Excellence in Architecture Award: Award of Merit

2003 Society of American Registered Architects, Design Award for Excellence

2003 *Texas Construction Magazine*, #1 Top Texas Project of 2003

E. Bronson Ingram College, Vanderbilt University (Nashville, Tennessee)

2019 American Institute of Architects Gulf States Region Honor Award

2019 Institute of Classical Arts and Architecture John Russell Pope Award—Commercial and Institutional Design

2019 Society of American Registered Architects Design Award of Honor

2019 Palladio Awards—Commercial, New Design and Construction, More than 30,000 Square Feet

Ed Smith Stadium (Sarasota, Florida)

2012 The Florida Chapter of the Institute of Classical Architecture & Art, The Addison Mizner Medal for Excellence in Classical & Traditional Architecture—Commercial

Firewheel Town Center (Garland, Texas)

2006 Texas Topping Out 2006, Top 10 Award

2005 Texas Construction Top 25 Projects of 2005

George Dean Johnson Jr. College of Business and Economics at the University of South Carolina Upstate (Spartanburg, South Carolina)

2011 The National Terrazzo & Mosaic Association, Inc., Honor Award Winner

Lon Evans Corrections Center (Fort Worth, Texas)

2013 Brick in Architecture Awards Competition, Gold Winner in Municipal/Government buildings

Maddox Muse Center (Fort Worth, Texas)

2001 Society of American Registered Architects, National Professional Design Awards Program, Design of Honor Award for Recognition of Superior Achievement & Professional Design Excellence

2000 Associated Masonry Contractors of Houston, Golden Trowel Award

2000 The Texas Masonry Council, Golden Trowel Regional Award for Design Elements and Craftsmanship

Merrywood Estate (McLean, Virginia)

1988 Landscape Contractors Association, DCA Landscape Architects, Inc., Environmental Landscape Award

Nancy Lee and Perry R. Bass Performance Hall (Fort Worth, Texas)

2008 Downtown Fort Worth Trailblazer Award, Placemaking

2007 The National Sculpture Society, The Henry Fielding Memorial Medal

2003 American Institute of Architects (Fort Worth Chapter), Excellence in Architecture Award, Citation Award

1999 The Chicago Athenaeum: Museum of Architecture and Design, The American Architecture Awards Program

1999 Masonry Contractors Association of America (Education/Government Category), presented to LUCIA for exterior stonework, International Excellence in Masonry

1999 American Institute of Steel Construction, Engineering Awards of Excellence Award of Merit

1999 Associated Builders and Contractors, 1998 Excellence in Construction, First Place

1998–99 *Holiday/Travel Magazine*, Travel Holidays 1999 Insider Awards

National Cowgirl Museum and Hall of Fame (Fort Worth, Texas)

2002 The Architectural Woodwork Institute, Award of Excellence

Parker Square Master Plan (Flower Mound, Texas)

2003 Society of American Registered Architects (California Council), Design Award of Merit

Penn Theater Project (Washington, D.C.)

1987 The Masonry Institute, Design Award

1984 Art Deco Society of Washington, First Annual Preservation Award

Private Residence (Utah)

2011 The National Terrazzo & Mosaic Association, Inc., Honor Award Winner

Private Residence/s (Washington, D.C.)

1990 Landscape Contractors Association, Grand Award—Environmental Landscape Award

1988 Landscape Contractors Association, Merit Award, Environmental Landscape Award

Sanger Lofts (Fort Worth, Texas)

2008 Downtown Fort Worth Trailblazer Award, Sustainable Development

1995 Historic Preservation Council for Tarrant County, Texas, 1995 Historic and Cultural Landmarks Commission Award

Sanguinet Building (Fort Worth, Texas)

2009 Downtown Fort Worth Trailblazer Award, Urban Design

The Saratoga (4601 Connecticut Avenue NW, Washington, D.C.)

1991 Society of American Registered Architects (SARA), Professional Design Awards Program

1990 American Institute of Architects, Architecture for Housing, Design for Living Design Award

1989 The Masonry Institute, Special Achievement Design Award

Schermerhorn Symphony Center (Nashville, Tennessee)

2014 Tucker Design Awards (Building Stone Institute)

2008 Real Estate & Construction Review, Gulf Coast / Tennessee, Plaque of Honor

2007 Tennessee Concrete Association, Design Awards Grand Champion

2007 Tennessee Concrete Association, Best Commercial Building, Large Producer Award

2007 Masonry Institute, Masonry Institute Award

2007 State of Tennessee American Society of Landscape Architects, Merit Award

2007 American Consulting Engineers Council of Tennessee, Engineering Excellence Honor Award

2007 Marble Institute of America, Pinnacle Award of Excellence

2007 Society of American Registered Architects, Design Award of Merit

2006 Associated Builders and Contractors, Inc. (Mid-Tennessee Chapter), Construction Awards of Excellence

2006 South Central Construction, Judge's Award for Best Overall Design

Schifter Residence (Private Residence)

2008 Society of American Registered Architects, Professional Design Award Honor

Severance Hall (Cleveland, Ohio)

2001 National Trust for Historic Preservation, National Preservation Award, for the sensitive restoration and expansion of Severance Hall, the world-famous home of the Cleveland Orchestra

2001 United States Institute for Theatre Technology, Inc. (USITT), Honor Award

2000 American Institute of Architects (Washington Chapter), Merit Award for Outstanding Achievement in Historic Resources

2000 The Cleveland Restoration Society, Preservation Award, Trustee Honor Award for Presentation Achievement

2000 American Institute of Architects (Cleveland Chapter), Certificate in Recognition of Exceptional Accomplishment in Areas of Preservation, Restoration, Adaptive Re-use and Maintenance of an Architecturally Significant Building

2000 Society of American Registered Architects, National Design Awards, Award of Excellence—Gold Ribbon

2000 Society of American Registered Architects (California Council), Design Award for Excellence

Sid Richardson Museum of Western Art (Fort Worth, Texas)

2011 Downtown Fort Worth Trailblazer Award, Preservation and Adaptive Reuse

2008 Associated Builders and Contractors, Inc. (North Texas Chapter), Excellence in Construction

The Smith Center for the Performing Arts (Las Vegas, Nevada)

2017 Society of American Registered Architects Design Award

2012 GE (General Electric Company), GE Edison Award of Merit for Lighting Design

2012 The National Terrazzo & Mosaic Association, Inc., Honor Award Winner

Southlake Town Hall (Southlake, Texas)

2001 United Masonry Contractors Association, Golden Trowel Award for Outstanding Craftsmanship in Residential and Other

Southlake Town Square (Southlake, Texas)

2000 Society of American Registered Architects (California Council), Design Award for Excellence

Sundance East (Fort Worth, Texas)

1997 Society of American Registered Architects, Design Award of Honor

1997 United Masonry Contractors, Golden Trowel Award, Outstanding Brick Design

Sundance East Comedy Club (Fort Worth, Texas)

2017 Architectural Precast Association Award for Excellence

Sundance 11 AMC Cinemas (Fort Worth, Texas)

1993 Associated Builders and Contractors, Excellence in Construction Award of Merit

1993 Associated Builders and Contractors, Outstanding Achievement, Excellence in Construction

1993 Illuminating Engineering Society International Illumination Design Awards, Edwin F. Guth Memorial Lighting Award of Excellence

1992 American Institute of Architects (Washington D.C. Chapter), Design Excellence

1992 Society of American Registered Architects, Design Award of Merit

1992 American Institute of Architects (Washington D.C. Chapter), Award for Excellence

Sundance Square (Fort Worth, Texas)

2018 Society of American Registered Architects Design Award of Merit

2017 International Making Cities Livable Design Honor Award

2014 Texas Topping Out Awards (EventLink Int'l), Top Award

2014 AIA|DC Chapter Design Awards, Award of Merit—Urban Design/Mater Planning

2014 Brick in Architecture Awards, Best in Class—Commercial

2014 CNU Charter Award, Best District

Sundance West (Fort Worth, Texas)

2008 Downtown Fort Worth Trailblazer Award, Sustainable Development

1994 Society of American Registered Architects, Design Award of Merit

Tarrant County Family Law Center (Fort Worth, Texas)

2006 Texas Topping Out 2006, Top 10 Award

2005 Associated Builders and Contractors – National Eagle Award

2005 Associated Builders and Contractors (Texas Chapter), Excellence Award—Institutional $25–99 Million

2005 Texas Construction Best Of 2005 Public Buildings

Texas Rangers Ballpark (Arlington, Texas)

1995 Associated Builders and Contractors, First Place—Excellence in Construction awards competition

1994 American Institute of Architects (Fort Worth Chapter), Recognition

1994 Society of American Registered Architects, Design Excellence

1994 *Dallas Business Journal*, Real Estate Awards, Best Community Impact-Architectural

1991 Texas Rangers Ballpark Design, Competition—Contract Award

The Waycroft (Arlington, Texas)

2020 Delta Associates Award—Best Washington/Baltimore Interior Design Apartment Community

2020 NAIOP Northern Virginia Awards of Excellence—Mixed-Use Project

The Westbrook (Fort Worth, Texas)

2017 Institute of Classical Architecture & Art John Staub Award—Institutional/Civic/Ecclesiastic/Multi-Family/Commercial Architecture

2014 United Masonry Contractors Associates, Golden Trowel Award—Commercial/Industrial

West Village (Dallas, Texas)

2005 Texas Topping Out 2005, Top 10 Award

2002 United Masonry Contractors Association, Golden Trowel Award, Outstanding Architectural Design, Residential & Other Winner

The Woodley (Washington, D.C.)

2018 Society of American Registered Architects Design Award of Merit

Worthington Hotel Renovation (Fort Worth, Texas)

1996 Society of American Registered Architects, Award of Merit

1996 Society of American Registered Architects, Design Award of Merit

1995 American Institute of Architects (Fort Worth Chapter), Certificate of Achievement

Yale University Environmental Science Center (New Haven, Connecticut)

2003 Society of American Registered Architects, Design Award of Merit

2003 Society of American Registered Architects (California Council), Design Award of Honor

2002 International Masonry Institute, New England Regional Golden Trowel Awards, Achievement in Architectural Design, Construction, and Craftmanship in Masonry, Outstanding Use of Masonry

PROJECT CREDITS

SPORTS & ENTERTAINMENT

The Ballpark in Arlington
Arlington, Texas
1991
Client: The Texas Rangers Baseball Club
Architect of record: HKS Inc.
Photography: Hedrich Blessing / Hall + Merrick

ESPN's Wide World of Sports Complex
Lake Buena Vista, Florida
1994
Client: Disney Development Company
Architect of record: HKS Inc.
Photography: Hedrich Blessing / Hall + Merrick

American Airlines Center
Dallas, Texas
2001
Client: Hillwood Development
Architect of record: HKS Inc.
Photography: Hedrich Blessing / Hall + Merrick

Dr Pepper Ballpark
Frisco, Texas
2003
Client: Southwest Sports
Architect of record: HKS Inc.
Photography: Hedrich Blessing / Hall + Merrick

Ed Smith Stadium
Sarasota, Florida
2011
Client: Sarasota County
Architect of record: Hoyt Architects
Photography: Hedrich Blessing / Hall + Merrick

Dickies Arena
Fort Worth, Texas
2020
Client: Event Facilities Fort Worth
Architect of record: HKS Inc.
Photography: Hall + Merrick + McCaugherty

OFFICE & RESIDENTIAL

1718 Connecticut Avenue NW
Washington, D.C.
1979
Client: Property Company of America
Architect of record: DMSAS
Photography: Fred Sons Photography (pp. 62, 65); Hedrich Blessing / Hall + Merrick (p. 64)

1133 Connecticut Avenue NW
Washington, D.C.
1989
Client: The Lenkin Company
Architect of record: Koubek Architects
Photography: Hedrich Blessing / Hall + Merrick (pp. 66, 68 bottom, 69); Ron Blunt Photography (68 top)

1201 F Street NW
Washington, D.C.
1990
Client: Carr America Realty Corporation
Architect of record: Page Southerland Page
Photography: Hedrich Blessing / Hall + Merrick

The Saratoga
Washington, D.C.
1986
Client: Horning Brothers
Architect of record: DMSAS
Photography: Hambright Hoachlander Associates (p. 74); Hedrich Blessing / Hall + Merrick (pp. 76–79)

The Woodley
Washington, D.C.
2014
Client: The JBG Companies
Architect of record: Cooper Carry
Photography: Hedrich Blessing / Hall + Merrick

13|U
Washington, D.C.
2017
Client: The JBG Companies
Architect of record: BBG-BBGM Architects and Interiors, PLLC
Photography: Hall + Merrick + McCaugherty

The Waycroft
Arlington, Virginia
2020
Client: The B.F. Saul Companies and Affiliates
Architect of record: WDG Architecture
Photography: Hall + Merrick + McCaugherty (pp. 4, 96–105)

MIXED-USE, RETAIL, & HOSPITALITY

Beringer Wine Estates
St. Helena, California
2001
Client: Beringer Vineyards
Architect of record: Architectural Resources Group
Photography: Hedrich Blessing / Hall + Merrick (pp. 108–113); David Wakely (pp. 114–115)

Sundance Square Master Planning and Buildings

Sundance West
Fort Worth Texas
1988
Client: Sundance Square Management
Architect of record: HDR
Photography: Hedrich Blessing / Hall + Merrick

Sanger Lofts
Fort Worth, Texas
1993
Client: Sundance Square Management
Architect of record: BOKA Powell
Photography: Hedrich Blessing / Hall + Merrick

Bank One Building
Fort Worth, Texas
2002
Client: Sundance Square Management
Architect of record: HKS Inc.
Photography: Hedrich Blessing / Hall + Merrick

The Cassidy & Trust Buildings
Fort Worth, Texas
2014
Client: Sundance Square Management
Architect of record: Bennet Benner Partners
Photography: Hedrich Blessing / Hall + Merrick

Sundance Square Plaza
Fort Worth, Texas
2013
Client: Sundance Square Management
Architect of record: Bennet Benner Partners
Photography: Hedrich Blessing / Hall + Merrick

Southlake Town Square
Fort Worth, Texas
2013
Client: Sundance Square Management
Architect of record: Bennett Benner Partners
Photography: Hedrich Blessing / Hall + Merrick (pp. 144 bottom left, 145); Hall + Merrick + McCaugherty (pp. 140, 144 top left, top right, bottom right, 146–147)

West Village
Dallas, Texas
2001
Client: Oak Creek Partners, Inc.
Architect of record: KSNG Architects, Inc.
Photography: Hedrich Blessing / Hall + Merrick

Firewheel Town Center
Garland, Texas
2005
Client: Simon Property Group
Architect of record: Beck Architecture
Photography: Hedrich Blessing / Hall + Merrick

The Linq
Las Vegas, Nevada
2013
Client: Caesars Entertainment
Architect of record: Klai Juba Wald Architecture + Interiors
Photography: Hedrich Blessing / Hall + Merrick

AC Hotel Spartanburg
Spartanburg, South Carolina
2017
Client: OTO Development
Architect of record: McMillan Pazdan Smith Architecture
Photography: Hall + Merrick + McCaugherty

Le Guanahani
Saint Barthélemy, French West Indies
Ongoing
Client: Le Guanahani
Architect of record: Bureau Xavier David
Photography: Hall + Merrick + McCaugherty

CIVIC, HEALTHCARE, & EDUCATION

Southlake Town Hall
Southlake, Texas
1999
Client: City of Southlake
Architect of record: GSI Architects, Inc.
Photography: Hedrich Blessing / Hall + Merrick

Tarrant County Courts and Criminal Justice Facilities
Fort Worth, Texas
2005
Client: Tarrant County, Texas
Architect of record: Gideon Toal
Photography: Hedrich Blessing / Hall + Merrick

Alpharetta City Hall
Alpharetta, Georgia
2014
Client: City of Alpharetta, Georgia
Architect of record: Smallwood, Reynolds, Stewart, Stewart and Associates, Inc.
Photography: Hedrich Blessing / Hall + Merrick

Cook Children's Medical Center
Fort Worth, Texas
Ongoing
Client: Cook Children's Medical Center
Architect of record: Karlsberger + Associates, Inc.; FKP Architects, Inc.; HKS Inc.
Photography: Hedrich Blessing / Hall + Merrick

Yale Class of '54 Environmental Science Center
New Haven, Connecticut
2001
Client: Yale University
Architect of record: GSI Architects, Inc.
Photography: Hedrich Blessing / Hall + Merrick

Hawken School Natatorium
Gates Mills, Ohio
2003
Client: The Hawken School
Architect of record: Collins Gordon Bostwick Architects
Photography: Hedrich Blessing / Hall + Merrick

George Dean Johnson, Jr. College of Business and Economics
Spartanburg, South Carolina
2010
Client: University of South Carolina Upstate
Architect of record: McMillan Pazdan Smith Architecture
Photography: Hedrich Blessing / Hall + Merrick

Vanderbilt University Residential Colleges
Nashville, Tennessee
Ongoing
Client: Vanderbilt University
Architect of record: Hastings Architecture Associates, LLC
Photography: Hall + Merrick + McCaugherty

CULTURAL

Nancy Lee and Perry R. Bass Performance Hall
Fort Worth, Texas
1998
Client: Performing Arts Fort Worth
Architect of record: HKS Inc.
Severance Hall
Photography: Hedrich Blessing / Hall + Merrick

Severance Hall
Cleveland, Ohio
1998
Client: Musical Arts Association
Architect of record: GSI Architects, Inc.
Photography: Hedrich Blessing / Hall + Merrick

Schermerhorn Symphony Center
Nashville, Tennessee
2006
Client: The Nashville Symphony
Architect of record: Earl Swensson Associates
Photography: Hedrich Blessing / Hall + Merrick

The Palladium
Carmel, Indiana
2010
Client: Carmel Redevelopment Commission
Architect of record: CSO Architects
Photography: Hedrich Blessing / Hall + Merrick

The Smith Center for the Performing Arts
Las Vegas, Nevada
2012
Client: Las Vegas Performing Arts Center Foundation
Architect of record: HKS Inc.
Photography: Hedrich Blessing / Hall + Merrick

Charleston Gaillard Center
Charleston, South Carolina
2015
Client: City of Charleston
Architect of record: Earl Swensson Associates
Photography: Hedrich Blessing / Hall + Merrick

Chapman Cultural Center
Spartanburg, South Carolina
2007
Client: The Arts Partnership of Greater Spartanburg
Architect of record: Little Diversified Architectural Consulting
Photography: Tim Buchman
Photography: (pp. 312, 315); Hall + Merrick + McCaugherty (p. 314)

National Cowgirl Museum and Hall of Fame
Fort Worth, Texas
2002
Client: National Cowgirl Museum and Hall of Fame
Architect of record: Bennett Benner Partners
Photography: Hedrich Blessing / Hall + Merrick

Sid Richardson Museum
Fort Worth, Texas
2006
Client: Sid Richardson Foundation
Architect of record: Hanfeld Hoffer Stanford
Photography: Hedrich Blessing / Hall + Merrick (pp. 320, 322 top left, 323); James Wilson Photography (p. 322 top right, bottom)

EMPLOYEES LIST

JOSE LUIS ABASTOS-MARTINEZ • MAYA ACKERMAN • ANATOLIY ADZHI-GIREY • LILLY AGUTU • MELISSA ALBERDING • MAYTHAM ALGHAFFARI • RAUZIA ALLY • ANNETTE ALMENDRAL • ALANA ALSOP • JOSE ALVAREZ • TOMAS E. ALVAREZ • MELISSA ANDERSON • ROBERT ANDERSON • ALEJANDRO ARANGO • VERA ARANGO • JOSH ARCURIO • RICHARD ARMINGTON • STEVE ARMINGTON • JASON ARNOLD • KIM ARRINGTON • ROSEMARY ARTHUR • BRYAN ASSON • ELENA ASTUA • EMILY ATWOOD • LAURENCE J. AURBACH • DANIEL AYAD • DAVID AYBAR • JASON BALECHA • PRADIPTA BANERJEE • SARAH BANNERMAN • JEFF BARBER • JASON BARRETT • FRANCIS BASOAH • JEFFREY BEAM • PETER BECK • MICHAEL L. BEIDLER • EYASU BELAY • MICHAEL J. BELISLE • MICHAEL C. BERRY • MELINDA BIEBER • PHILLIP BLEVINS • SUSAN BLOCK • BRANDON BOBACK • JOHN BOLIG • CARMEL BONFIGLI • ISAAC BONILLA • ERIK BOOTSMA • DOUGLAS BOTHNER • CARY C. BRADFORD • DAVID BRAWNER • JILL I. BRETHERICK • TORYN BROADWATER • MARK VAN BROCKLIN • ROBERT BROOKS • BELLAMY BROWN • CHRIS BROWN • SHEILA K. BROWN • RICHARD D. BROWNING • JOHN BRYANT • MARK BUENAVISTA • CAROLYN BURELBACH • SARAH T. BURNHAM • ALEXANDRA BURR • JORDAN CAHILL • JON CAKERT • ABRAHAM R. CALHOUN • STEPHANIE CALLAGHAN • KRIS CALLORI • CURTIS CAMPAIGNE • DOUGLAS CAMPBELL • FREDY ABELLA CANAS • AMANDA P. CANNON • CHAD CARNAHAN • DOUGLAS CARNAHAN • EVELINE CARPENTER • JENNY CASTRONUOVO • JULIA CASWELL-DAITCH • CHRIS CAYTEN • AMY CHANG • WAYNE CHANG • MERCEDES CHAPARRO • ANDREAS CHARALAMBOUS • CAITLIN CHARTIER • DALLAS CHAVEZ • KRISTIE CHIN • PIZZI CHRIS • SANDRA J. CLARK • JENNIFER CLYNCH • STEVEN COBB • KEITH COHN • MICHELLE COHN • KRIS COLLINS • DENNIS CONNORS • M. NOEL CONNORS • TOBIE CORBAN • ROWENA CORBETT • KAREN CORRALES • MARY CUK • PETER CUNNINGHAM • EMILY CURATO • JULIA DAITCH • COLGATE W. DARDEN • BLAIR DARGUSCH • JACK DARNELL • JULIE DAVIS • MARK E. DAVIS • WARREN DAVIS • ALYSSA DEADY • TIMOTHY S. DEAL • ISABELLA DEBENEDETTI • BROOK G. DENISON • DAVE DERENICK • MONIKA DEW • ROBERT DEW • SARA DEWEY • TAKSIT DHANAGOM • THEODORA DIAMANTIS • LINDSEY DICKES • ALEXANDRA DICKSON • CHARLES DIDCOTT • PATRICK DIGIOVANNI • ANTHONY DIMANNO • MARCOS DOMINGUES • MARIO DOMINGUEZ • CHARLES DONAHUE • LINDA DONNARY • THOMAS DOUGHERTY • NANFO DOWNS • KAREN DRAZIN • AVA DUGO • PENELOPE DUNN • STEPHEN DUPONT • EVAN DZIEDZIC • SCOTT EDMONSTON • ANDREW EDWARDS • ESTELA EDWARDS • KAMILAH EDWARDS • JANE ELLIOT • MARK ELLIOTT • WILLIAM H. ELLIS • ALLAN ENCARGUEZ • ALICE ENZ • VIRGINIA ESCALONA •

NORMA ESCOBAR • SPENCER ESPLIN • KATHRYN EVERETT • SHERI FABIAN • MONIQUE FAGGANS • RAMSAY FAIRBURN • ZAINAB FAISAL • RUTH FANUEL • TIMOTHY FARINA • VIVIAN M. FERNANDES • GEORGE D. FILLION III • MARGARET FLINNER • ELIZABETH FLOYD • JENNIFER FLYNN • GREGORY FONSECA • MATTHEW FORD • JONATHAN S. FOSTER • DOUGLAS E. FOWLER • SEBASTIAN FOXLEY • NAOMI FRANKLIN • HUGH FRASER • FORREST FRAZIER • ANNE FREEMAN • CRAIG M. FRIEDMAN • PAUL R. FRIETAG • DAVID FRUZYNSKI • DIANA FULFORD • ELIZABETH FULLER • LISA GARCIA • SONIA GARCIA • LISA GARCIA-TZAREFF • SARAH GARDNER • KATHRYN GARRETT • RYAN GEBHART • MICHAEL GERDING • LAUREN GILMARTIN • PAUL GLOTH • MILES GLOVER • JULIAN GOLDMAN • HOLLY GOMEZ • ANGELINA GONZALEZ • JOSUE GONZALEZ • MARIA GONZALEZ • MEGAN GONZALEZ • BETH GOTTFRIED • NIMA GOVIND • ANDREW GOWER • JORDAN E. GRAVES • MATTHEW GREENBERG • PHILLIPS GREENE • THOMAS H. GREENE • JUAN GUARESCHI • SCOTT GUENTHER • LOUIS CREATH GUILLOT • JOHN HADLEY • SUSAN HAINS • TRISTAN HAMILTON • JACK R. HARRINGTON • VALERIA HASBUN • DAVID HATHCOCK • DAVID HATHWAY • MARSHA HEARD • TERRESA HEINZ • RICHARD HELLEBRAND • JENNIFER HELLER • BRIAN HENDRYX • MONICA HENRY • JON HENSLEY • MANNIX HERNANDEZ • FRANCISCO HERRERA • JOHN F. HERRINGTON • JOHN HERRINGTON • NICOLE HINKLE • GUY HODGES • MAGGIE HOLSINGER • MARKUS HONGMANIVANH • STEVEN HORWITZ • GREGORY HOSS • KIANA HOSSEINI • MARK HOUSE • TED HOUSEKNECHT • JEFF VAN HOUTEN • GREGORY HUGHES • COURTNEY HUNT • HARRY HUNTER • DAVID HYMES • MATT IRETON • SUSAN IRVINE • FERDOUSI ISLAM-AMIN • EMILY JACKMAN • ERIC JACKMAN • PAUL JACKMAN • SCOTT JAFFA • MAURISSA JENNINGS • GENEVIEVE JERYGA-LAURVA • DOUGLAS JOHNSON • MICHAEL JONES • VANESSA JONES • WILLIAM R. JONES • GLORIA JORGE • JOHN JORGE • DOUGLAS KANE • DAEWHA KANG • MAXINE KARAM • JOAN KAUFMAN • DAVID N. KAY • ROSS KEARNS • PATRICK J. KEATING • PATRICK KEETLEY • J. ANDREW KELLER • COLLEN KELLY • ELIZABETH KELLY • KACI KEPFERLE • AMY KESSLER • ANGELICA R. KETCHAM • MEGAN KINDLE • MICHAEL KIRK • BRANDON KISER • MALGORZATA KIULIN • STEVE KNIGHT • ERIC KOM • MEAGHAN KROENER • JOHN KUCIA • JOSEPH KUNKEL • MARISA KURTZMAN • YEE LAM • PALMER LANE• PAUL LANGLAND • MANUEL LAUZURIQUE • GEOFFREY LAWSON • WILLIAM LEACH • DOUG B. LEE • JOHN LENKIN • JACQUES LEVET • MEGHAN LEWIS • CORNELIUS IVES LISTER JR. • STEVE LIZARDI • GARY LOCKREY • GREGORY LOMAN • JEFFREY LOMAN • MICHELLE LOPEZ-ORSINI • CHRIS LYON • JOHNNY MAAS • GLENN MACCULLOUGH • BERNADO MACHADO • JEREMY MACK • BEN MADDOX • PATRICK MAHAR • LEAH MALITO • W. CLARK MANNING • COREY MANNO • YOLANDA MARINA • DEREK MARKS • MIRELA MARMARA • JERRY MARSHALL • LESLIE E. MASON • NASIR MASOOD • LISA MATEY • WAMBAA MATHU • CAMDEN MCCLELLAND • ROBERT MCCLURE • ASHLYN MCKEITHAN • MAUREEN MCKERON • BERT MEEKINS • JOSE MEZA • MELISSA MILEFF • AMANDA MILLER • TRAVIS MILLER • LUKE MOLINELLI • BILL MONET • JUAN MORENO • MEGARAN MORRIS • DAN P. MOSELEY • JONATHON H. MOSS • FIONA E. MUELKEN • GABRIELLE M. MUISE • STEVE MULLINEAUX • ELENA MURPHY • JULIAN MURPHY • RASHIDBEK MUYDINOV • ABDUL MUZIKIR • JOHN NAHRA • JOHN N. NAMMACK • ZARA NASER • NATHANAEL NELSON • PATRICK NELSON • MATT NEUMANN • CHARLES NEWBURN • MATT C. NEWBURN • SEAN NOHELTY • JOHN J. NOLIS • STEVEN K. NOSE • HAYES NUSS • CARA O'BRIEN • BRIAN O'LOONEY • BEN OLSEN • KELLY O'MEARA • MATTHEW M. OSSOLINSK • RONALD OSTEZAN • ALEXA OSWALD • ASHLEY OZBURN • ANDREW PACKEY • ALLISON PALMADESSO • JENNIFER PALOSKI • LUCAS PARKER •

STEVE PAYNE • ROLAND O. PEPIN • ELDAMARIA PESCHIERA • JAMES E. PESCIO • THERESA PETRAMALE • STACEY PHILLIPS • TODD S. PHILLIPS • JOEL PIDEL • PIER D. PIERANDOREI • JULIA PILIPOVICH • CHRIS PIZZI • MATTHEW POE • LUIS G. PONS • RHIANNON PORTER • WILLIAM POULOS • JUAN PRIETO • FAITH PRIMOZIC • HEATHER PRIPSTEIN • LISA Y. QUINLIN • JAMES RAMSEY • JOSEPH RAPAZZO • ERIC REBBERT • PETER REIGER • MEGAN REINECCIUS • DEAN REINEKING • JON A. REINHARD • COLE REMBECKI • DONNA RENDELMAN • JUAN RESTREPO • DIANA S. REUTER • JOHNATHAN RICH • LIANI RICHARDSON • ANNA RICKERT • PATRICK RIORDON • ARIANE RISTO • JON ERIC RITLAND • NOEMI B. RIVIERA • KIMBERLY A. ROLLINGS • CASEY ROOT • ALLYSON DEL ROSARIO • ELENA ROTH • STEPHEN M. SAFF • PEDRO SALES • IVA SALLER • CHRISTOPHER SALVADORE • MUHAMMADALI SAMI • BRUCE W. SANFORD • TEREZA SCHAIBLE • RHIANNON SCHROTH • DAVID M. SCHWARZ • JEFFERY SCOTT • WILLIAM SEATH • ELIZABETH T. SHEPARD • VALERIE SHERRY • EVAN G. SIEGEL • KIMBERLY P. SIMONS • SANDRA SIMPSON • THOMAS SINCLAIR • BJORN SLATE • MARY K SLEVIN • SANDRA SMART • DERRONDA SMITH • ISAAC SMITH • KEN D. SMITH • PAULINE SMITH • CHUN KIT SO • TIMOTHY SO • JESSICA SOFFER • SALLY SOHN • JEFFREY SOZIO • SEAN STADLER • LAUREN STARK • DAVID J. STASS • CHRISTOPHER STEWART • ZACHARY STEWART • JON STILES • JENNIFER STINSON • THOMAS J. STODGHILL • STEPHEN STRASSER • MIKE SUTTON • MICHAEL SWARTZ • MARK TALBOT • SHALINI TANEJA • HEATHER TARNER • MICHAEL TAYLOR • BARRIE TEACH • CHRISTOPHER TEIGEN • KEN TERZIAN • JEFFERSON B. THOMAS • ADRIANE THOMPSON • BRENNA THOMPSON • ERIK THOMPSON • LAURA THOMPSON • CHRISTINE TIFFIN • METAYA TILAHUN • KENT TITTLE • MAJA TOKIC • ROLAND TOMASSO • ROBERT TONDO • JON TOONKEL • CHRIS TORRES • JANE TREACY • HANNAH TSIMMERMAN • RASHAWN TUCKER • HASAN H. UCAK • VIVIAN URIBE • SEBASTIAN VANDERBECK • JAMES M. VANDERPUTTE • JOEL VANDERWEELE • JEFF VANHOUTEN • KYLE VEATER • TOMMY VINCE • ERICA VINSON • CATHERINE VISEN • PHILLIP WAGNER • STEFANIE WAHL • DOUGLAS WARD • EMILY WEN • MAGDA WESTERHOUT • WILLIAM WHITE • KRZYSZTOF WIACEK • JASON WILCOXON • DANIELLE WILKENS • CRAIG P. WILLIAMS • DANIELLE WILLKENS • JEFFREY WILSON • CHAS WINEBRENNER • EVAN WISKUP • ALEX J. WITKO • HANA WOLDEAMANUEL • MARK E. WOUTERS • KANGXIN WU • HUGH XU • LAURA YDROBO-COLMENARES • JOY YODER • KALOYAN YORDANOV • RICHARD ZAMBITO • MOJGAN ZARE • ALEX ZBOROVSKIY • TERRY ZINK • JON G. ZUBILLER • LAUREN E. ZUZACK

Published in Australia in 2024 by
The Images Publishing Group Pty Ltd
ABN 89 059 734 431

Offices

Melbourne
Waterman Business Centre
Suite 64, Level 2 UL40
1341 Dandenong Road
Chadstone, Victoria 3148 Australia
Tel: +61 3 9561 5544

New York
6 West 18th Street 4B
New York, NY 10011
United States
Tel: +1 212 645 1111

Shanghai
6F, Building C, 838 Guangji Road
Hongkou District, Shanghai 200434
China
Tel: +86 021 31260822

books@imagespublishing.com
www.imagespublishing.com

The Images Publishing Group Reference Number: 1607

NATIONAL LIBRARY OF AUSTRALIA
A catalogue record for this book is available from the National Library of Australia

Title: David M. Schwarz Architects: Forty Years // Text by Craig P. Williams
ISBN: 9781864709148

This title was commissioned in IMAGES' Melbourne office and produced as follows:
Editorial Georgia (Gina) Tsarouhas, *Art direction/production* Nicole Boehringer
Thanks to Helen Koehne (proofing)

Printed by Graphius nv, Belgium, on 150gsm GardaMatt Ultra art paper

FSC www.fsc.org MIX Paper from responsible sources FSC® C014767